A to Z Virtues

26 Powerful Exemplars of Virtue

Chaz E. Allen

Published by Challenge My Family, 2019.

A TO Z VIRTUES

First edition. October 6, 2019.

Written by Chaz E. Allen.

For Sara. Ever since the moment that I met you, I can divide my life into a before and after...

CONTENTS

Introduction

A spark, that's all this is. This book had high ambitions in the beginning, but as I invested more and more of myself into its production, I realized that I am wholly inadequate to the task of fully fleshing out the amazing stories of these characters. Each short story highlights a moment in the life of someone who embodied a virtue. From Nelson Mandela's benevolence during truth and reconciliation in South Africa to the grit of Audie Murphy in World War II, these are stories to which every child should be acquainted.

Still, I am an amateur author and the depth and nuance of these historic figures exceed my ability to capture in writing. Nonetheless, if even one of these short stories—works of historical fiction—can spark a desire for learning in the heart of a child, I will consider the whole venture a resounding success.

I once heard a story about ancient Greece that has always stuck with me. The story goes something like this. At the games in Olympia, an old man was searching for a seat among the throngs of spectators. Every spot was taken, so the old man searched and searched. Some Greeks in the crowd jeered and insulted the old man for blocking their view. None offered him kindness. But when he arrived before the Spartans, all of the boys and many of the men arose and yielded their seat to the elderly fellow. With tears in his eyes, the grey-haired man made a biting observation.

"Alas for the evil days! Because all the Greeks know what is right and fair, but the Spartans alone practice it."

It seems to me that the challenge is not knowing the difference between right and wrong, virtue and vice. No, the true test is in the doing of things, the application of virtue in everyday life. How often are we told to be truthful, studious, and productive, and how more often still do we find ourselves drawn to the temptation of idleness or unearned leisure.

We need heroes. We need examples of what right looks like. We need to see a principle put into action and observe the consequences. The farmer's law is immutable and eternally true.

"You reap what you sow."

What is the harvest of a life well-lived? We can look to Patton, Regulus, and Helen Keller who reaped fruits of audacity, integrity, and thankfulness. What is the outcome if we persevere, and live nobly, with zeal? Ed Coan, George Washington, and Amelia Earhart show us.

They say you sow a thought; you reap an action. You sow an action; you reap a habit. You sow a habit; you reap your character. You sow your character; you reap a legacy. I hope to see my children and this whole generation reap a legacy worth reading about, a legacy of virtue and hope.

Lastly, I offer a note to parents. Some of these short stories include violence and themes that may seem too mature for young ears. I leave it to you to decide which stories to tell, feel free to modify them as you see fit. I abstain from profanity (with one exception), because I want children to learn that they can express themselves articulately, without using crass terms.

You will also find some words well beyond the elementary level. That too was deliberate. I want to expand the vocabulary of the younger generation. We use words to bring life to our thoughts and more words at our disposal means we can convey our thoughts in more rich and meaningful ways. If a word is bold, its definition appears at the back of the book—a glossary of sorts.

Many of the individuals highlighted in this book have aspects of their past that are less than perfect. Patton was arrogant, Franklin a philanderer, Washington a slaveholder, and so the list goes on. The examples I chose hail from a variety of nations, races, and walks of life. It was a deliberate effort to show that examples of virtue are found in every corner. There is at least one thing that they have in common.

Every single person featured herein (except Jesus Christ—of course) is human, which means each one made mistakes, yet still tried to live a noble life. We can relate to them, learn from them, and choose to seek the virtues they embodied.

I am not a professional writer, nor a historian. But, I have tried to do my due diligence as I built the profile of each character. Where possible, I used their own words to fill their dialogue. In some cases, I filled in the gaps with what my imagination told me they would say. To help you differentiate between actual quotes and my narrative, I have placed quotes in italics.

The major themes, locations, statements, and events are real, inspiring, and far more interesting than I present them here. I encourage every family to read a short story, talk about the virtue in question, and then discuss how their child can apply it in his or her daily life—whether that be in school, on the soccer field, or at home. Hopefully, your child will want to do some additional research into the life of that hero.

It was a delight putting these stories together. Each night, after completing a story, I would read it to my children as they prepared for bed. In their excitement to learn more, they bombarded me with questions. My answers and our subsequent discussions on how to live like our heroes brought me great joy. I hope your family enjoys these stories as much as my own.

Now, go ahead, sit back, relax, find a comfy spot on the couch with your kids. Get ready to transport them into a wild and inspiring world, long ago in a land far, far away.

Best,

Chaz E. Allen

1. AUDACITY of Patton

Intrepid boldness, strong confidence in yourself.

"L'audace, l'audace, toujours l'audace!" ("Audacity, audacity, always audacity!") – Napoleon Bonaparte

Bastogne, Belgium 1944

SURROUNDED. THAT WAS what the lieutenant said about a week ago. German forces had surrounded the city and sent the command post a message demanding surrender. The lieutenant said General McAuliffe had given a one-word reply over the radio, "*NUTS.*"

Staff Sergeant Welker smiled as he thought of that **laconic** response, a witty reply from the old man. Of course, he wouldn't surrender. His chest puffed up with a bit of pride for the Airborne; he still felt like his Troopers were the best stuff the American Army had to offer. He was a Screaming Eagle, of the 101st Airborne Division.

All of that running, drilling, jumping out of airplanes, patrolling, and shooting back in the states wasn't for nothing, he knew that. Shoot, as far as Welker was concerned, there was no doubt every one of his boys would rather fight to the very last bullet than walk into one of those Nazi POW camps.

Besides, he had already heard rumors of what the **SS** were doing to American prisoners at Malmedy, there was talk of American doughboys getting formed up against a wood line and mowed down by machine guns.

Buried in a shallow grave—didn't sound pleasant.

He hoped that maybe a few were able to get away, to escape into the vast Ardennes forests. There were so many trees, a man could definitely hide out there, evade the enemy.

The cold though, the **forsaken** chill that sinks deep—freezes your very soul—would find you even if the Germans didn't. No, even running away into the woods sounded like a miserable end. December in Germany was not at all the pleasant Christmas experience he longed for.

With teeth chattering, he vowed he would never again sing any songs about a "White Christmas."

He could hardly believe Christmas was just yesterday. Welker had tried to bring some Christmas cheer to the fellas, but it was already nearly a week into the siege and best he could do was cover a bunch of his men's guard shifts. If he couldn't give them a proper gift or warm meal, he could let them catch some shut-eye and maybe dream of such luxuries. For some reason, these small acts of service made Welker smile, it made him feel pretty good, the spirit of Christmas or something like that.

He supposed he should feel lucky, he had an extra pair of wool socks that didn't even have holes in them. He was excited about putting them on as soon as his watch came to an end. Sure, his toes (actually everything) seemed wet and numb right there and then in the foxhole, but soon enough Corporal Jacox would be crawling up to relieve him and he would be able to creep back to the comfortable rubble of Bastogne where his platoon was set up.

It wasn't even much of a city anymore, almost every building was shattered; it was a surreal landscape. He wondered how many American soldiers were buried in that rubble, crushed or blown to bits. His squad was still in decent shape, the first few days were the worst, that was when they lost Billy and Drake right before his eyes.

One second they were firing away on the .30 caliber machine gun, cutting through the advancing German soldiers and the next they were gone. The explosion had knocked everyone on the line down into their holes, dirt and chunks of wood flying in every direction. Welker had clawed himself to the top of his hole and was calling to his squad, getting them back on the guns, when he looked to his left and saw Billy's position—at least what used to be Billy's position—transformed into a crater.

Oddly, for a second it looked just like those craters his dad had shown him with that telescope he liked so much. One clear night, back home, he and his dad got a good look at that moon. Bastogne's mottled gray snow and ever-cloudy sky reinforced the lunar image.

It just seemed so **arbitrary**, who lived and who died.

Welker was able to regroup his squad and hold the line, but only barely, and at great cost. Since that day he felt lucky that their sector hadn't been pressed again with such ferocity.

Probing attacks, of course.

Artillery incessantly.

But no major attacks.

Dry socks though, that's all he wanted, some nice dry socks.

"STAFF SERGEANT WELKER, hey sergeant, I'm coming up." Corporal Jacox's whisper seemed to carry farther than it should in the darkness. The slight rustle of cloth on branches confirmed that his relief was crawling his way up to the foxhole. Welker was going to be glad to have the company. Jacox slid into the hole and the dawn's early light glinted off the young soldier's toothy grin.

"You think it'll be today sarge? The boys are saying that ol' Patton is going to be rolling in soon, that he is marching a whole Corps on the double. You think we are finally getting out of this stinking pit?"

Jacox's breath turned into a pale mist as he spoke, "Nothing against Bastogne, mind you, but this winter vacation is getting old. You know, it ain't quite as pretty as them pictures in the brochure." Jacox was always able to bring humor to a situation.

He was just about to laugh at good ol' Jacox's sarcasm when he heard the low rumble of engines and the breaking branches of trees under tank treads. His eyes narrowed as he looked out into his sector and was just about to tell Jacox to shut his trap when the sky erupted.

Mortar rounds and artillery shells bloomed out of the earth in every direction. The only thing that kept their soft flesh safe from the hail of white-hot shrapnel was Welker diving on top of his corporal sinking them deeper into their cramped foxhole.

"Return fire! Get to your positions! This is it boys, they are pressing the line!" Welker's yell seemed to mute with every explosion, but his squad heard him and were already working their rifles and machine guns. It wasn't easy finding targets in the dim light, but shooting toward muzzle flashes seemed to work.

Panzer and Tiger tanks were rolling in, their metal armor clearly **impervious** to Welker's small arms. He called for his

Bazooka team, they needed to get those tanks or his whole line would be rolled over in minutes. The German infantry accompanying the tanks were taking a beating, if he could keep his belt-fed machine guns going, he might just have an opportunity for a shot at the lead Panzer.

The bazooka team was bounding from Welker's position, just a few more yards and they would be at the spot he had assigned them to engage the German tank. Tragically, a line of tracer fire cut the bazooka team down right before they reached cover. Welker pounded his fist into the ground, "No! that was our one shot."

Jacox gave his squad leader a friendly jab in the shoulder, "It's okay sarge, I owe ya one for covering that guard shift back on Christmas. Just keep their heads down for a second."

Before Welker could protest, Jacox was out of the hole and running for the Bazooka, his boots kicking up clumps of slush and debris. All of his men fired on the advancing Germans, suppressing the infantry screen for a critical moment.

The bazooka's blast rang out and sounded weak compared to the overall din of the battle, but the bazooka's rocket sank right into the Panzer's flank and exploded in a flash of light. Less than a second later, flames from the blast caused additional explosions to ring out from within the tank as its rounds started cooking off. Welker's squad gave a yell of excitement at the sudden stroke of luck. He looked over to Jacox, crouched behind a half-demolished brick wall, and could see his white teeth as he smiled back at him.

Then the second Panzer fired its 75mm main gun. Jacox and the entire wall he was hiding behind exploded into a plume of dust. The Germans began to regain their momentum.

Welker felt crushed, he didn't have anything left to throw at his attackers. He had just lost his last bazooka and three of his finest men, his friends who had jumped into Normandy with him during operation **Overlord**, only a few months ago. It seemed like a lifetime.

His machine gun crew yelled for more ammunition; he knew there wasn't any. His team leader was calling for a medic, but there was no way a litter team would be able to make it to their position before the Germans. It was too much. Everything was stacked against him; the end was inevitable.

But Welker was a Screaming Eagle, and this was the 101st Airborne, and no German was getting past his line while he and his men drew breath. He pulled his trusty M1 carbine up to his shoulder and started squeezing the trigger.

Then, another clatter crept through the trees, it was the sound of engines and men, by the hundreds. But these engines were different than the low growl of the German Tiger, it was the Sherman Tanks of Patton's Third Army!

Welker could hardly believe his eyes as tanks of the United States 4th Armored Division crashed through the trees into the open field, guns blazing. The German attack faltered and then collapsed into confusion as American GIs flanked the German line. Not a single Panzer or Tiger tank managed to retreat from the field, the burning husks spat clouds of black smoke into the already cloudy winter sky.

Jacox had been right after all. Patton had made it.

DESPITE IMPOSSIBLE odds, old "Blood and Guts" had managed to turn his forces in France north and move hundreds of miles to attack with two full divisions within forty-eight hours of hearing about the Nazi attack. The Germans feared and respected Patton more than any Allied general. During D-Day, multiple German divisions were kept over 150 miles to the Northeast of Normandy because they feared Patton might land at Calais.

Patton was a wealthy man and could easily have left the Army for a life of leisure, especially after valiantly fighting during World War One. Yet, Patton loved the military and craved the opportunity to lead men into battle. He led his forces with strict discipline and maintained a tempo that kept the Germans continually on the ropes. Patton, with some theatrical flair, offered the following counsel.

"It is foolish and wrong to mourn the men who died. Rather we should thank God that such men lived."

"If everyone is thinking alike, then somebody isn't thinking."

"A good plan violently executed right now is far better than a perfect plan executed next week."

"Never tell people how to do things. Tell them what to do and they will surprise you with their ingenuity."

"Better to fight for something than live for nothing."

Audacity appeared many times during the Battle of the Bulge. The 101st audaciously refused to surrender, individual soldiers boldly faced a superior German foe. But Patton's drive north to save the paratroopers was most audacious of all. He risked exposing vulnerable flanks and outrunning his supplies over heavily forested terrain, in the dead of winter so that he could expedite his movement north. Patton's audacity and leadership ensured the rescue of those brave Screaming Eagles.

2. BENEVOLENCE of Mandela

The quality of being well meaning; kindness.

"Courageous people do not fear forgiving, for the sake of peace." -Nelson Mandela

Cape Town, South Africa 1995

M andela pressed his brow with his fingers, the headache wasn't going away. He muttered to himself, "Truth and **Reconciliation**, hmm, maybe the name should have been, **Quagmire** of Moral Uncertainty."

The apartheid was over, his revolutionaries had won, a new government was in place, and he was the president. Still, behind the initial thrill of victory, there was an emptiness. The unmistakable reality that many people, innocent people, had died to bring this change about. He knew the cause was worth it, but the cost still felt high, and the land was still boiling with ill-will.

A knock sounded at the door.

Archbishop Desmond Tutu entered, his purple cleric tunic brightly contrasting the man's weathered expression. "If you don't mind, I hoped to share the results of some of today's proceedings."

Mandela smiled despite the headache, "Yes, yes, of course, you know you are always welcome in my office. How did things go today? How many petitions have we seen now, is it 6,500?"

"Over 7,000 Mr. President, with stacks more to go. We have granted over 800 petitioners amnesty and refused more than 5,000. Some accuse us of bias, of heartlessness, and prejudice against our white brothers. Others accuse us of being too lenient against those that persecuted and subjugated our black brothers. We are walking a fine line between justice and mercy. Well, stumbling down the line is probably a more suitable expression." Tutu responded.

"Yes, we have been successful so far—unquestionably—in at least one manner old friend," said Mandela.

"What might that be, Mr. President, the end of the **Apartheid**?" asked the Bishop.

Before he answered, the President drew in a slow breath and the word *Apartheid* rang in his ears. Apartheid was the Afrikaans word for "apartness." It was the South African government's sanctioned racial segregation. It was a discriminative policy that lacked even the empty rhetoric of America's, "separate but equal," stage. It guaranteed non-whites remained squarely under the boot heel of the white minority.

Separate bathrooms, faucets, park benches, entrances, any excuse to exclude non-whites came to **fruition** during the Apartheid. 1948's National Party still saw the African natives as a natural resource, ripe for exploitation, a holdover from colonial times. Who else would endure the brutal labor in the many lucrative gold and diamond mines? Slavery may have officially ended, but little had really changed.

The Defiance Campaign's boycotts, strikes, and non-violent protests against the utter-unfairness of the system yielded no change. If anything, the resulting police brutality and mass arrests only deepened the **schism**.

Mandela would never forget the sixty-nine dead protestors at Sharpeville. Outrage—that old familiar sensation—started to build in his gut. They were mere protestors. The violence preyed upon them by the state was cold-blooded murder. That was the day that broke Mandela, it shattered his hope for peaceful reform. The sight of those lifeless, innocent bodies burned into his memory and fueled a need to end the injustice.

Paramilitary operations were not pleasant. The next year he sought vengeance through action, calloused to collateral damage. For him, he was fighting fire with fire, violence against violence. Some called it terrorism, they may have been right. He called it his only option. Yet, when he was arrested for treason, he knew he could expect no mercy from the government. Twenty-seven years of prison proved that correct.

"MR. PRESIDENT? YOU were about to say something?" Tutu looked inquisitive.

"Yes, yes, indeed I was. I was just thinking. We have been successful in something. Something I had a lot of time to consider while I was imprisoned on Robben Island. That little patch of land taught me much. You know, it's only about five miles from here, just that direction." Mandela pointed out his window.

"Eighteen years I was there. I know because I kept track of every single day." His voice sounded distant.

"Every day I looked at the walls of my cell and drew in the scent of the ocean. I liked that about the island, no matter how dank the cell, the smell of the ocean made its way to you. The whole island is less than two square miles, the entire thing could fit in one of the other prisons I had the pleasure of visiting." Mandela breathed in deeply.

"Small island, small enough for a man to think about his place in the world." He looked down at his desk.

"It used to be a leper colony. Did you know that? Lepers." Mandela rubbed at his arms.

"You know how I found out? The guards told me. They said that lepers walked the same rocky paths I was walking, that they segregated themselves to the island, many of their own accord. They did it because they knew they were different, that they were defiled, a walking **plague** on society."

He looked up at the Bishop, "The guards were oddly authoritative on the disease. They described in gory detail how the leper's limbs deform, ulcers burst upon the skin, and that the bacteria would slowly eat the person alive."

The next words slowly left his lips, "They said I was a leper, that my people were the new plague destroying society."

The Bishop started to interject, but Mandela shook his head, "You know what, in one small—but very important way—those guards were not wrong. I also learned that lepers often died of unnoticed wounds, of repeated injuries and infections that nerve damage had masked."

After a pause, Mandela looked up at the vaulted ceiling, "You see, they lacked the ability to feel pain. Just like me. After Sharpeville, after seeing our people confined in poverty and squalor, I felt nothing but rage."

"I commanded our Spear of the Nation Paramilitary Group. We sabotaged and destroyed over 200 government buildings. We were relentless. My later capture and sentence of high treason further fueled the hate inside me. But after years, decades, in that tiny cell, I grew numb. I felt nothing but emptiness."

He eyed the Archbishop humbly, "I became an emotional leper. When I was released from prison, the joy I felt was muted by the realization that the same emotional plague had stricken our entire nation. Non-whites wanted vengeance and retribution from the Europeans, and the whites seemed entrenched in their bigotry."

Mandela stood from his desk and faced the window. "Violence and retribution, we couldn't have that. Truth and reconciliation were the only way forward with any promise. Those who felt they had been a victim of violence could finally be heard. Those who carried out violence would be able to give testimony and request amnesty from prosecution. Here we are, thousands of petitions later, and we are still embroiled in the process."

The Archbishop joined Mandela at the window and they looked out at the bustling port city of Cape Town, its markets shadowed by Tabletop Mountain in the distance. The chairman felt Mandela's hand clasp him on the shoulder as they both gazed out on their beautiful nation.

"Yes, my friend, we have been successful in one critical way. We have begun to wipe the plague of emptiness and hatred from our souls. We have started down a path of empathy, forgiveness, and reconciliation, and one day we may just feel love for each other once and for all."

NELSON MANDELA CONTINUED to serve as South Africa's President and helped it transition to a democratic state committed to the rule of law and respect for human rights. He taught the following important truths.

"It always seems impossible until it's done."

"No one is born hating another person because of the color of his skin, or his background, or his religion. People must learn to hate, and if they can learn to hate, they can be taught to love, for love comes more naturally to the human heart than its opposite."

"I am the master of my fate: I am the captain of my soul."

"I never lose. I either win or learn."

Benevolence proved to be a hallmark of Mandela's Presidency. He had the opportunity to condemn the former white government leaders. Instead, he chose a higher path and sought to work with those who were once his enemy. He truly cared about the long-term success of his nation. Mandela was benevolent.

3. CANDOR of Hackworth

The quality of being frank, open, and sincere.

"If you don't like something, don't snivel or whimper about it. Sound off – express your views – be prepared for the consequences." -Colonel David Hackworth

65 Kilometers North of Fire Base Danger, Vietnam 1969

Raindrops splattered onto the barrel of his M16 rifle. It was coming down in sheets now, the ground was already soft and might soon turn into a pit of mud and muck. At least it wasn't the rainy season; this was probably an isolated storm. They shouldn't be cut off from air support for too long.

Lieutenant Colonel "Hack" Hackworth looked up and squinted against the incoming rain. Yes, if his senses were right, they were definitely going to be needing air support.

"Sir, point man says he saw enemy movement up ahead, he has halted the patrol and we are setting up immediate security. What do you want us to do from here? Should we press forward and try to flush them out?" Lieutenant Marek's fresh, too-young face looked at him intently.

"Hold position. We need to make sure this isn't a baited **ambush**; the Vietcong (VC) have been known to draw us in and then cut us down with artillery and machine guns. Their bunkers are so well-concealed we barely know where it comes from. Get our M60s set up on our patrol's apexes and have two squads push out along our flanks. I'm calling brigade to let them know what's going on." Hack gave the young LT a thumbs up and shooed him away.

Specialist Wyatt crouched next to his Battalion Commander, "Sir, I've got Brigade on the net; they want to know why we have halted."

Hack grimaced and accepted Wyatt's hand microphone, "This is Recondo-Six actual, over."

"What's the holdup? You were told to advance through Sector Bravo and push the Vietcong into Third Battalion's kill zone. Hammer and anvil, Recondo-Six, YOU are supposed to be the doggone hammer. What good is a hammer if it refuses to swing, over?" The frustrated voice came through the handset surprisingly clear.

"Understood, sir, I have two squads reconnoitering right now. We have established contact with the enemy, but we need to make sure we are not walking right into an ambush." Hack kept his voice cool; he had a hard time getting along with his new brigade commander. He was one of those ticket-punching (doing things to check the block) U.S. officers, more interested in furthering his career than anything.

"NEGATIVE. Get your men moving, that's an order, over," was all Hack received in reply.

"Sir, weather rolled in, we don't have eyes in the sky right now, no air support. Not to mention, this air assault was so far into the highlands that we are on the very limit of our howitzer's range. Unless you can guarantee me priority from division artillery, I'm not sending my boys into a possible meat grinder. Did we learn nothing from last week?" Hack released the press-to-talk switch.

The rain was not letting up, Wyatt shifted under the weight of his radioman's rucksack as water poured off his helmet in a stream. He remembered last week. A whole platoon raced into the jungle, hot on the heels of a scurrying Vietcong soldier.

Not a single American soldier emerged alive.

"This operation is a direct response to that last mission. We have them right where we want them. So help me, Recondo-Six, you order your men forward this instant or I'll send someone in who will. UNDERSTOOD? Acknowledge Recondo-Six, over." Hack could picture the old full bird, staring at a map in his operations center miles and miles away from danger. He was probably surrounded by his minions, coffee in hand, clean as a whistle in his dry fatigues.

A new voice crackled into the radio.

"Sir, this is Chaos-Six actual, we have enemy movement on our front as well. My soldiers are ready to move. We humbly request a change of mission, sir; we are glad to assume hammer duties. I'm sure the Recondos will be glad to sit tight and let us drive the enemy right to them, over." It was none other than Lieutenant Colonel Kyle Massendell, a West Pointer, and the commanding officer of Chaos Battalion.

Hack didn't have anything against academy grads. Lieutenant Marek was a West Pointer too and was a combat-proven leader, respected by his platoon, and reliable in battle. The problem with Massendell was that he was an **obsequious** "Yes Man."

During a casual encounter at the officer club, Massendell had revealed that he had his eyes on public office after the war. He said Vietnam was the perfect place to build his resume, and with any luck, he would come home with a decoration or two. Hack felt he was one of those shallow **dilettantes** who ran from pillar to post trying to punch their card, serving minimum time in combat to limit real exposure. Hack never heard him mention pride in his soldiers or commitment to the overall mission. Not surprising either, Chaos Battalion was aptly named.

In Chaos, soldiers had no regard for dress and grooming standards. The bunks in their quonset huts were surrounded by pornography and smelled of marijuana. Bottles of alcohol were strewn about, alongside random links of ammunition. The Chaos firebase looked like a gypsy camp.

The junior officers refused to enforce standards because they cared more about popularity than they cared about doing what was right. Hack gritted his teeth at the thought of it, he wished he could show those officers that the cost of their popularity was the readiness of their men. He was glad his Recondo leaders chose the higher path, they would not needlessly lose lives, even if it cost them popularity.

"Approved as requested Chaos-Six. Recondo-Six, hold your position and set up the anvil. Await further orders, over" replied the Brigade Commander.

Hack keyed the microphone, "Sir, request we allow my recon teams to report the enemy's disposition. This could be a trap and we are about to send a whole lot of dismounted infantry right into it, over."

Chaos-Six interjected on the net, "I disagree, sir, there is no way the Vietcong could have set up something so elaborate in so little time. At most they might have a few elements of the North Vietnamese Army (NVA) with them. We have the numbers, I am confident we can destroy their entire formation with ease, over."

Hack came back on, "Sir, the fact that intel confirmed the presence of the NVA should give us pause. We have no idea how many NVA infiltrated into these jungles; it could be a few companies or it could be an entire division. I need five more minutes for my reconnaissance report. Tactical patience, sir, if we waltz in there, we will be finding out the hard way, sir we need to..."

"ENOUGH." The commanding officer cut into the transmission, "Chaos-Six, press the attack. We need to seize the initiative, fix the enemy, and destroy him. We will not let Charlie get away this time, I don't want anyone to escape. Give me a complete body count no later than 2000 hours, I need to report our progress up to General Westmoreland. Carry on the mission, out."

Body count. How could we be measuring success with the number of enemy killed? Were we in a medieval war of attrition? What was it now, 50,000 or more U.S. service members killed in these jungles? Sure, the VC and NVA were paying a heavy toll in lives, but Hack knew many of the numbers reported to Washington were inflated—or in many cases outright lies.

A patrol would come back and say they killed two NVA soldiers. Brigade would hear that and assume that if two were confirmed killed then another four or five dead must have been dragged off by their comrades, so they reported seven. Division saw the report and made the same assumption, so seven became fifteen. By the time the numbers were passed through the echelons and arrived in Washington, two had become two hundred.

Thus, as far as the Pentagon was concerned, we were winning, because we had killed upwards of 900,000 NVA and VC while we had only lost 50,000.

Only 50,000. The thought made his stomach turn. Minutes ticked by until a sudden roar filled the jungle a few kilometers away.

"LIEUTENANT MAREK, COME here son." The well-built Platoon Leader bounded to him with **alacrity**.

"The Battalion is supposed to be setting up the anvil, and Chaos Battalion advanced about ten minutes ago. Our recon elements confirmed what I feared, the NVA is here in force. They managed to identify heavy machine guns and at least a battalion's strength of fighting positions, and that was just on our immediate front."

"My guess is they have two brigades holed up in this mountain. You can hear the firefight; they have us outgunned, and they know it. The point is, Chaos walked right into that firestorm, and our line of sight radios can no longer reach them." Hack grabbed the boy's shoulder.

"Chaos is in there right now getting chewed up. We can't let that happen. We must expand our line and fix the NVA right in their trap, not let them escape. Then we will drop Arty, napalm, and everything else in our cookbook right on those rascals. Recondo elements are already spreading into position. But Chaos is cut off without an exit, and we need them out of there before we call it all in." He loaded a fresh magazine into his M16.

Hack's somber face revealed the gravity of what he was asking, "I need you to take your platoon and fight your way through to Chaos. We have no air support, and we can't start dropping artillery anywhere but our immediate front, or we will hit American G.I.s. You need to cut Chaos an exit. You'll be outnumbered and advancing against an entrenched enemy, but in about 15 minutes we are going to **raze** the entire mountain. You are their only hope."

"We got this, sir, just give us some covering fire and we will move out. We will get to them. *HARDCORE RECONDO,* Sir"! Marek squared his jaw and was off in a flash.

"*No slack,*" replied Hack. He knew it was probably the last time he would see the young man again.

ON JUNE 1971, COLONEL Hackworth appeared on ABC-TV's *Issues and Answers.* Calmly, Hack told the American viewing audience that the U.S. military strategy in Vietnam was bankrupt. He decried the body count method of assessing success and addressed the unacceptably high number of "friendly fire" casualties in which Americans were accidentally killing other Americans. He ridiculed the training that left U.S. recruits ill-equipped to fight a guerrilla war and described the South Vietnamese military leaders as corrupt.

Knowing full-well that speaking the truth during the interview would mean the end of his aspiring career and forfeit any chance of becoming a general, Hack still spoke candidly. He was one of America's most decorated soldiers, who had performed valiantly in Korea and Vietnam. He transformed dysfunctional units into crack formations of troops.

He offered the following mentorship. *"Bravery is being the only one who knows you're afraid."*

"Respecting your opponent is the key to winning any bout. Hold your enemy in contempt and you may miss the strategy behind his moves."

*"If a policy is wrongheaded, **feckless** and corrupt I take it personally and consider it a moral obligation to sound off and not shut up until it's fixed."*

"You can't make a unit proud by praising it and you can't make a soldier proud by telling him how tough or good he is. That's the superficial stuff. No pain, no gain. They had to earn it."

"Leadership is not a popularity contest."

Candor set Colonel "Hack" Hackworth apart as a warrior who cared more about his men and the success of the mission than his career or personal safety. He fought for what he felt was right and never allowed himself to become a "Yes Man." He was brash, uncouth, and sometimes arrogant, but through it all, he was a man of candor.

4. DISCIPLINE at Rorke's Drift

The ability to control yourself, even in difficult situations.

"An army is a fighting weapon molded by discipline and controlled by leaders; the essence of the army is discipline." – Bernard Montgomery

Rorke's Drift, South Africa 1879

Lieutenant John Marriott Chard wiped at the dusty sweat on his brow as he looked at the burning hospital and what was left of his men. Over a thousand British regulars—nearly the entire field Army—were lying dead just a few miles from here at Isandlwana. Lieutenant Henderson's 100 horsemen had managed to retreat in good order from the massacre, arriving at Chard's outpost only hours ago. His report was not promising.

Henderson revealed that over 20,000 Zulu warriors had engaged the main column and that at least 4,000 Zulu were headed toward Chard's position at Rorke's Drift. Chard knew he had to hold his outpost or risk slaughter.

Initially, he was glad to have Henderson's native horsemen; they desperately needed their strength to bolster the meager number of 141 British soldiers at the outpost. That hope evaporated though when Henderson's men fled after the Zulu's first charge.

What had he said? Oh yes, *"his men would no longer obey his orders."* Perhaps they had seen their fill of death for the day, no sane man would want to again face the Zulu's man-killing spears. No regular man would stand when certain death stared him in the face and his knees trembled in fear.

Alas, Lieutenant Chard did not command regular men. He led crack British Troops, **steeled** for battle, and equipped with courage born of hard discipline. Henderson's men fled while Chard's men stalwartly manned their posts.

"Color Sergeant Ammon, collapse the perimeter, bring all the men into the bastion. The sun is setting and we cannot remain strung out; this fight is far from over." Chard returned the crisp salute of his trusted senior enlisted officer.

As Ammon brought the men into their meager fortification of last resort, Chard reluctantly counted the dead and wounded. The fighting had been raging since early afternoon and although he was glad the numbers were not worse, each of the lifeless ten bodies before him tore at his heart.

They needed every man if they were going to survive the night.

"What is the situation with our ammunition, color sergeant?" Chard knew they had started the day with approximately 20,000 rounds, but they had leveled volley after volley at the Zulu for more than six hours.

Ammon checked in with his squad leaders, "Aye, sir, I wish I had better news. We only have approximately 5,000 rounds left. The squads have divided the remaining ammunition amongst themselves and have established their sectors of fire. The perimeter is thin, many are wounded, but as long as we can rapidly redistribute ammunition and men, I be confident we will hold, sir."

The sun dropped below the horizon and darkness gathered. The stars Acrux and Becrux of the Southern Cross shone like pinpricks of light in the purple **firmament**. Chard still marveled at the African landscape. It was nothing like his home back in London. The very constellations in the heavens here were foreign. At least the moon was familiar.

His wife, Sara, told him she would send a wish to the moon every night they were apart. They began the tradition years ago when he was on his first voyage in the queen's armada. Since then he would long for the moon's rise and spare a moment to think of her. But this night the Eastern horizon was an empty, inky black.

Color Sergeant Ammon reloaded his rifle next to his lieutenant. "It's darker than a Glasgow alley, sir. Could this **fell** day not even give us the simple pleasure of a full moon?" He chuckled to himself ironically.

"What, and go and make things easy on us? I am afraid you have not been paying attention, color sergeant. No, the whims of fate will be affording us no special favors this night. At least, none that we can count on." Chard tried to sound casual.

"It will be the discipline of the men that sees us through," said Chard.

"Don't know about that, sir. Seems to me like we have already been smiled upon this red day. Why, the fact that we have men still living and breathing under your command at all is a bit of a miracle." Then Chard caught Ammon's wink in the dim light.

Chard replied, "If it's a miracle, color sergeant, it's a short-chambered, Boxer-Henry .45 caliber miracle."

Ammon's wink turned into a full grin, "And a bayonet, sir. With some guts behind it. Speaking of bayonets, the boys have all fixed them. Without much illumination to speak of, we lose our ability to engage the Zulu at range. It is going to be a close-in fight, we cannot afford to be wasting ammunition firing blindly into the night."

Then, seriously, the color sergeant added: "We've placed torches at twenty-five and fifty meters, we will not pull the trigger until we can see the whites of their eyes."

"HERE THEY COME!" THE **picket's** yell put the entire perimeter on full alert. Suddenly, materializing out of the darkness in an instant, thousands of Zulu warriors charged past the first line of torches. Their *assegai* short spears and cowhide shields casting violent shadows on trampled earth.

Chard stood atop the bastion's structure and held his saber high. The saber was a symbol of his position, the mark of his command. His subordinate officers kept their sabers in their scabbards so that every man knew to look to Lieutenant Chard. His orders ruled these final hours and there would be no confusion on their task.

"HOLD STEADY. Await my command." Grizzled British men shouldered their rifles.

The Zulu advanced impossibly fast, already almost to the second torch line. Tall and muscular, the Zulu warrior was capable of nearly ripping a man limb from limb. Armed with his spear and beside his brothers, the Zulu was more than a formidable adversary. Chard respected the discipline of the Zulu, had it not been for his picket they could have crept up to the very walls undetected. They had made no sound at all, thousands of them.

"Ready, make every round count. Aim. FIRE." Chard sliced his saber down through the air and fired his pistol into the oncoming horde of screaming Zulu. The entire perimeter erupted in a flash of exploding powder and ball. Nearly the entire front line of Zulu warriors collapsed under the volley.

Where those warriors fell, more took their place and the endless advance continued.

"Maintain the line. Give them all you've got lads! Third squad, send four men to the West Wall, they are beginning to collapse." Color Sergeant Ammon's Scottish accent managed to cut through the din of battle and four men swiftly repositioned themselves on the barricade. Like a war horse following the reins of its rider, the Soldiers heard and obeyed their leader's commands despite the chaos.

The Zulu were at the barricade now, climbing on top of one another to gain purchase on the wall. The bayonets were taking their toll on the advancing force, but from Chard's perch, he could tell it was only a matter of time before a hole in the line developed. As he lowered his revolver to hastily reload an idea struck him.

"Color Sergeant, have we any black powder left? I need a barrel." He was running to Ammon's position.

"Sir, what? Oh, yes, I believe we do. Here it is, one barrel. What could you possibly want to do with it? Things are a bit busy on the line, as I am sure you are aware, sir." Ammon was discretely cradling an *assegai* wound to his arm.

The battle had reached a decisive point; his men were exhausted; their ammunition was low. Their discipline held them in their positions and his second echelon of defenders was able to cut down the few Zulu who had thus far made it over the perimeter.

That would not last though, he could feel it in him, years of exposure to battle had honed his senses and somewhere deep within him, he knew that the next few seconds would decide the night. His father had been a soldier and told him that a leader's place was in the front, assuming the same risk and hardship as his men, that the leader had to be present at the decisive moment.

This was that moment at Rorke's drift.

LIEUTENANT CHARD GRABBED the barrel and was off. He **deftly** maneuvered it to the West Wall where the Zulu had been massing. He could tell it was where they intended to finally break through and flood the yard.

"Make way! Give me a lane!" The British soldiers had no time to even look over their shoulders. They recognized the voice of their commander and peeled open a lane, even as they continued to fight the Zulu. The lieutenant hurled himself into the fray, immediately being stabbed by an *assegai* in the side, then the leg, then sliced along his face.

Despite the frenzy, Chard still managed to light his alcohol-soaked cloth and insert it into the powder keg right before casting the whole thing over the wall into the undulating swarm of shrieking warriors.

WHABOOM!

With a blinding flash, instantly pitch-black night became fiery day. The blast created a crater of flesh and limbs, Zulu warriors prostrate in every direction. Fire spread across the ground like a blossomed sunflower.

Chard had been too close when it went off and was blown back into the perimeter, his once-crisp red uniform now charred with blood and dust. His ears were ringing and the whole world spun overhead. There on his back, he could not tell if the stars he saw above him belonged to Africa or his own shattered senses.

Still, he could tell his men were taking advantage of the sudden distraction and had renewed their efforts to clear the wall. The Zulu were falling back, the softening sound of their footsteps testifying their retreat.

"Sir, that was a bloody wild idea you had there." Ammon had come forward and was cradling the head of his wounded commander. "If you were gonna go and do a thing like that I would have thought you'd have had the decency to invite me along." He smiled down at his trusted leader, blood from their wounds blending into their red uniforms.

"How is the line? How many of the men are...were any...we need to..." Chard couldn't decide what to say, everything was still jumbled in his mind.

"Don't you worry about any of that, sir. The lads know what to do. They are cleaning up the perimeter and redistributing ammo as we speak. See, look at them go, you should be proud, sir." Ammon directed the lieutenant's gaze to the perimeter. Then, with a pause, he lifted his view to the horizon.

"And look at that, sir, wouldn't you know it? It looks like the moon is rising after all, a full one at that. We are going to have a bit of light around here for a change, maybe there is room for a few more miracles this night."

Chard managed a smile as he looked at the rising moon. He smiled in pride for his men and their bond of discipline in action. He smiled thinking of his ever-witty color sergeant. Mostly, he smiled at the thought of his wife, Sara.

THE BATTLE OF ISANDLWANA marked the worst defeat British forces ever received at the hands of an indigenous foe. Rorke's drift would have been just another massacre in an already black day, but Lieutenant Chard's brave few held strong. They continued fighting through the night and preserved the outpost. Hundreds upon hundreds of Zulu dead were strewn across the field while only seventeen British soldiers fell in the long battle. Discipline enabled the small force's success.

"Discipline is the soul of an army. It makes small numbers formidable; procures success to the weak, and esteem to all." – George Washington

"The temptation to take the easy road is always there. It is as easy as staying in bed in the morning and sleeping in. But discipline is paramount to ultimate success and victory for any leader and any team." -Jocko Willink

*"Discipline is based on pride, on **meticulous** attention to details, and on mutual respect and confidence. Discipline must be a habit so ingrained that it is stronger than the excitement of the goal or the fear of failure."* -Gary Ryan Blair

"No man is fit to command another that cannot command himself." -William Penn

Discipline manifested itself on both sides of the Anglo-Zulu war. The Zulu were able to organize and employ a vast field army better than any other indigenous group. They maneuvered silently and trusted their leaders with their lives. The British soldiers relied on their years of discipline, self-control, and training as they held the perimeter at Rorke's drift. They reloaded with precision and obeyed commands with exactness. Of all the factors that enabled their survival, the decisive element was certainly discipline.

5. EQUANIMITY of Bogle

Mental calmness, composure, evenness of temper.

"Time is your friend; impulse is your enemy." -Jack
Bogle

Valley Forge, Pennsylvania 2008

"SELL, we need to sell everything related to the housing industry. The market is crashing all around us and any stocks we own in mortgage lenders will destroy our index returns. We have got to split the index and sell, Jack. I'm not overstating it when I say this situation is apocalyptic for our company." The senior executive's anxiety spread like a contagion among the board members.

Almost overnight, the United States stock market was crashing and there seemed no bottom to its fall. Many speculated that it was the dawn of another great depression. Talk of sky-high unemployment, foreclosures, bankruptcies, and vaporized retirement savings was reaching every household.

Jack Bogle, Chief Executive Officer of the Vanguard investing group, leaned back in his chair. He would not pretend that the market's sudden turn did not make him nervous. The talk of Great Depression struck him particularly deep. At 79 years old, he was one of few still living that survived those dark years. He was just a kid at the time. He and his twin brother David had never even heard of markets and stocks, they couldn't begin to grasp the international economy.

But they did know things were bad.

The yelling, the threats, the sobs and the despair that they heard coming from their parents' bedroom all started soon after their Dad lost his job. At first, he and David enjoyed having their Dad home. He even came into the backyard and threw the ball with them a few times. But it didn't last long.

Soon their father was shrouded with desperation and self-contempt. One night, Jack and David eaves-dropped on a muffled argument where their father accused their mom of having no self-respect for sticking with a loser who couldn't even find a job. The boys were introduced to a new word the next morning—Divorce.

It didn't take long to figure out what that word meant.

THE SENIOR EXECUTIVE continued, "Jack, the index fund is your invention. It has revolutionized investing. What was that quote from Wall Street? Oh yeah, '*this Bogle invention stands alongside the invention of the wheel, the alphabet, and the **Gutenberg press**.*' There can be no higher praise. You cut operating expenses like no one thought possible and eliminated all risk of greedy fund managers and unnecessary fees. But even you could not remove all risk from the equation. Our funds are plummeting in value."

"That is correct, Frank." Jack looked up at the board members with his hands clasped in front of him. "I certainly stand by the idea that *owning the stock market over the long term is a winner's game, but attempting to beat the market is a loser's game.* That has not changed, even with the current volatility."

"Volatility? Jack, VOLATILITY? This is a dumpster fire; we need to call it like it is here. No one is coming out of this unscathed. You realize our company is built almost entirely on indexes that track the entire market?" The executive stood from his chair and leaned into the table.

"Did you hear me? The entire market...and the entire market just jumped off a cliff." His face was turning red, but no one could tell if it was due to frustration or desperation.

Jack leaned forward and cradled his chin with his fingers. He could feel stress like he had known in his younger years boiling up inside him. He needed to bring calm to the situation, but he could feel his heart increase its cadence.

It still felt odd knowing the heart wasn't even his.

HE REMEMBERED THE FIRST time he felt an unusual pressure build in his chest. He had come home from a stressful day at the office. He and Eve had just said goodnight to their six children when Jack felt a squeezing sensation on his left side. In a moment, it evolved into a piercing pain. His chest, back, even his neck suddenly gripped with an intolerable ache. His chest hurt so bad, breathing came in short weak breaths.

At first, he thought he might just be over-reacting, maybe dealing with some simple acid reflux. After all, Eve had served some pretty spicy chicken earlier that day. But that didn't explain the profound sense of fatigue that suddenly coursed over him.

The last thing he remembered was Eve rushing toward him as he collapsed to the ground.

"Arrhythmogenic right ventricular dysplasia," that was what the doctors called it. The doctor could have used English and simply stated that he had a weak heart, that if he wasn't careful more heart attacks would follow. Eventually, he would need a heart transplant.

Eve wasn't convinced his condition was a rare genetic disease. She blamed all of the stress Jack was subjecting himself to on Wall Street. He was an outspoken critic of the equities industry, claiming that, "*on balance, the financial system subtracts value from society.*"

None of his colleagues appreciated the critique. Jack saw them grow rich off of their investors, taking a commission on every trade and reaping a percentage of each portfolio, regardless of its performance. All too often the mutual funds they managed failed to beat the market, yet they continued to line their pockets.

"You're too uptight, Jack. This is how it has always been and always will be. We help our investors grow their wealth; their money is better in our hands; shouldn't we be compensated for our hard work?" His peer pulled keys from his tailored suit, rolled his eyes, then called Jack a white knight before he drove away in his Lamborghini.

To Jack, it seemed unethical, taking the hard-earned cash of their clients and **frittering** it away on unnecessary trades. He knew many of the investors were small-town families hoping to have some money available in retirement. If the excessive fees weren't bad enough, the exorbitant salaries of the Wall Street executives were untenable.

Only a few years before, the compensation for a chief executive officer (CEO) was already an extravagant forty-two times that of the average worker. Now, it was around 500 times greater. Yet, somehow CEO compensation was rising 8.5 percent annually while regular workers enjoyed a negligible increase. They rationalized it saying they had "created wealth" for their shareholders. But were CEOs actually creating value commensurate with their huge increase in compensation?

As far as Jack was concerned, absolutely not.

Their lavish lifestyles would not survive scrutiny as the market drew the public's eye. Jack was determined to provide the average worker an opportunity to invest at little cost, to eliminate the middle man and purchase shares that reflected the entire market.

Eve knew he was giving every ounce of his energy to the effort and his health suffered as a result. Jack, on the other hand, was willing to accept that he'd been dealt a tough hand, even when five more heart attacks followed. Eventually, he was blessed with a heart **transplant,** and he refused to let his second shot at life go to waste.

"Yes, Frank. I heard you." Jack also took to his feet, his older frame suddenly swelling with **vitality**. "I heard you loud and clear. Make no mistake. I am precise in my speech. Volatile is exactly the word to describe the market, here in 2008 and twenty years from now. You must *remember that success in investing depends in part on your character and guts, and in part on your ability to realize at the height of **ebullience** and the depth of despair alike that this too shall pass.*"

Jack looked at Frank, then turned his gaze to meet the eyes of each of Vanguard's board members. "This too shall pass. Mark my words; *this company will continue to rely on the ordinary virtues that intelligent, balanced human beings have relied on for centuries: common sense, thrift, realistic expectations, patience, and perseverance.* We will not allow ourselves to be pulled into rash decisions because of passion or fear. Amongst our senior leadership and down to our newest investor *we need to recognize that the two greatest enemies of the investor are expenses and emotions."*

Frank deflated a bit and sat back into his chair, but doubts remained. "What if we fail to act and don't have any investors left?" He gestured with his hands, "What if—poof—this whole company tanks and ceases to exist. Not all of us donate half of our salary to charity like you, we have bills to pay."

Jack's expression softened. There it was. Fear and a drive for self-preservation, both a result of warped perspective. "I understand your feelings. When my brother and I were trying to earn work scholarships to afford to go to school, we could barely see beyond the next semester's bills. Princeton taught me much, but it couldn't teach me the most important lesson. It took a heart transplant to teach me that."

The board room was silent, a sudden reverence swelled for the man standing at the head of the long table. "After my surgery, I considered each day a gift. I enjoyed the beauty of a sunrise and the giggle of my grandchild like it was as rich and perfect as imaginable. I learned to be in the moment, but to still work with a long-term view."

"When you abide by your core principles and keep your sights set on your legacy, you appreciate the now while never forfeiting the future. Vanguard will ride this storm and emerge stronger than ever. If not, never forget the words of Marcus Aurelias, *"very little is needed to make a happy life."*

VANGUARD WEATHERED the financial crisis of 2008 and rose to become the largest issuer of mutual funds in the world, with over $5,000,000,000,000 assets under management. Jack Bogle insisted on receiving one of the lowest salaries on Wall Street and never compromised on his desire to bring wealth to average workers. He said, "The miracle of compounding returns has been overwhelmed by the tyranny of compounding costs."

"Don't look for the needle in the haystack. Just buy the haystack."

"The greatest enemy of a good plan is the dream of a perfect plan. Stick to the good plan. Traditional."

"When there are multiple solutions to a problem, choose the simplest one."

Equanimity was a mark of Bogle's legacy. He refused to let passions rule his actions and kept his composure even in the most trying of circumstances. Vanguard's triumph was built on equanimity.

6. FRUGALITY of Franklin

Quality of being economical with money; thriftiness.

"A penny saved is a penny earned."-Ben Franklin

Philadelphia, American Colonies 1775

The red coat soldier eyed the incoming gentlemen with scrutiny. Unrest was spreading through the colonies and talk of **secession** was no longer confined to dark corners. British loyalists were harder to come by and his soldiers roamed the streets with trepidation. "Good evening, sir, may I ask what business you have at this establishment?"

Ben Franklin pulled off his hat and gave a slight bow. "Good evening to you as well, Captain. I appreciate your interest in my affairs. I tell my children, *either write something worth reading or do something worth writing.* Today, though, I'm afraid its simple business here at the exchange. I must pay off a few debts, nothing worth writing about if you ask me."

The captain blushed at Franklin's candor, "I apologize for intruding on your personal affairs, sir. The garrison is under orders to surveil certain prominent Philadelphians. I explained to my superiors that you are more philosopher than revolutionary, but they insist. I hope you understand."

Franklin chuckled, *"Never ruin an apology with an excuse,* Captain. I understand and offer no complaint. You are doing your job as well you can." He shook the soldier's hand and bid him adieu.

The door jingled as Franklin crossed the threshold. The man behind the counter nodded at him and in a hushed voice said, "You are here early, good sir. I suspect your counterparts will not be arriving at my back door for another fifteen minutes."

"I needed a few minutes to prepare my thoughts. You know, if you fail to prepare, you are preparing to fail and all that." Franklin sidled up to the counter and withdrew a small leather purse. "Besides, I needed to repay you for those books on the Enlightenment you secured for me."

The storekeeper accepted the money and jabbed at Franklin, "Honestly, I don't know how you can find any entertainment in such dry literature. Are you a **glutton** for reading punishment? You didn't have to pay me back so quickly by the way; I know you are good for it."

Franklin feigned insult, "*We are all born ignorant, but one must work hard to remain stupid,* my friend. Those books may just supply the ethos upon which this nation builds itself. You already know my affinity for the practical values of thrift, hard work, education, and community spirit, but we also need the scientific and tolerant values of the Enlightenment."

He started to make his way to one of the back tables and said over his shoulder, "I insist on paying you back promptly, debt is not a burden I subject myself to lightly."

THE BACK DOOR CRACKED open and two men entered, the first was tall and so elegant he nearly floated to Franklin's table. The second was short, stout, and resembled a bull trying to be quiet in a china shop. "Mr. Jefferson, Mr. Adams, I am pleased you were willing to meet with me so promptly. I do hope your arrival was unmolested by **unscrupulous** red coats."

Jefferson placed a hand on Franklin's shoulder. "You are very kind to worry about our well-being. Old John and I are becoming somewhat skilled in elusiveness. Why, I was just saying to John that when we got here we needed to express our gratitude for your hospitality and..."

Adams interjected, "Fine, fine, I believe the time for pleasantries is long past gentlemen. For what purpose do we find ourselves here, barely outside the prying eye of his Royal Highness, George III?" Adams never was one to mince words. Some found his abrupt nature off-putting, but Franklin found it endearing. No polite veneer masked ulterior motives with Adams.

"Indeed, yes, right to it then, we must advance to the next step toward independence. Thus far, we have toyed with ideas, bantered about possibility, and sewn seeds of interest in the ideals that could forge a great nation. But up to this point, all we have are words and clandestine conversations. *Well done is better than well said* and it is time for action." Franklin's jovial face was suddenly stone-cold serious.

"Just what kind of action do you intend?" Adams looked skeptical "We have been able to keep this movement a secret so far, but incautious action could place our whole network at risk. The penalty for treason, hmm, what was it again? Come on Mr. Jefferson, would you remind me?"

"Death." Jefferson said under his breath, his face pale.

Franklin held up three fingers. "*Three may keep a secret, if two of them are dead.* If you honestly believe this movement for independence remains a secret then I may have to reconsider my esteem of your intelligence, Mr. Adams. Honestly, you are the last person I thought I would need to convince that *they who can give up essential liberty to obtain a little temporary safety deserve neither liberty nor safety."*

Adams frowned and leaned in toward Franklin, placing his muscular forearms on the table. "Well now, Mr. Franklin, it sounds to me like you really are serious about this whole endeavor."

Suddenly a grin cut across his lips, "It is about bloody time." He pointed at Jefferson, "I have been trying to get this fine gentleman here to spare some time from his plush couch at his Monticello estate and commit to revolution. So, what is this next step you recommend?"

"There must be legitimacy to this revolution. It cannot be a power grab by the wealthiest members of the colonies. You both know me and are familiar with my works as an author, printer, scientist, and inventor. Of all my ventures my favorite has been inventing, but when it comes to creating this new nation, we cannot just invent ideals out of whole cloth."

Franklin's words filled with passion. "America must build itself on eternal principles, self-evident truths, and unalienable rights. It is the only way to ensure her success."

A British soldier walked past the storefront and the three men attempted to act natural.

"Just what are you getting at, Mr. Franklin? We here at this table agree that life, liberty, and the pursuit of happiness are God-given rights to every man. But, what kind of government will be able to make that possible? Will this new land extend those rights to everyone, regardless of wealth, race, or gender?" Jefferson looked genuinely interested in an answer.

Franklin looked back at his friends, "I do not know the answer to that. Everyone should be given an opportunity to succeed, that much is certain. We have a long way to go to see that realized, but I am confident that one day all Americans will enjoy freedom and quality of life beyond what we can now imagine. *With thrift, ingenuity, and integrity this nation will rise up like a beacon.* But still, it must first become a nation and for that, we need a declaration of independence."

Adams rocked back into his chair. "Well, finally we come to the meat of it. You are saying we need to craft a statement that tells old George III that his precious little colonies are no longer his to molest. I like it. In fact, Jefferson, you should write it. You always were good with words, even if they are a bit flowery for my taste."

"Wait, gentlemen, one moment, please. You think I am capable of producing such a manuscript? I certainly am eager to do my part, but this is no small matter. This must be done right, be completely beyond reproach. It will be the first step in unifying the colonies into a single nation." Jefferson looked a bit overwhelmed by the task.

Franklin rose from the table and came around to the other two, placing his hands on their shoulders. "The declaration is only the first step. We will have a war to win. King George III is not going to allow our departure without contest. Later we will need Articles of the Confederation, or a Constitution, to truly unite these disparate colonies into a whole, E Pluribus Unum gentlemen."

"Out of many, one." Adams's gruff exterior **belied** his affinity for languages, he was fluent in French, German, and Latin.

"Exactly," said Franklin. Then he was off toward the door, leaving his comrades in contemplation.

HE WALKED DOWN THE path of his beloved Philadelphia, almost everyone he passed greeted him warmly. Franklin had a reputation for being generous and kind. Most folks knew he was the wealthiest man in the city, but he never flaunted his riches. Even as his business ventures soared, he remained grounded and preferred the company of regular workers to the powder and wigs of old money and high society. He was eager to share wisdom and taught, *"Tell me and I forget, teach me and I may remember, involve me and I learn."*

"An investment in knowledge always pays the best interest."

"Instead of cursing the darkness, light a candle."

"Be at war with your vices, at peace with your neighbors, and let every new year find you a better man."

Frugality helped Franklin rise to riches in colonial America and then use his considerable resources to enable the revolution. He was economical in his spending and conscientious in his dealings with his fellow men. He was a colonial-era renaissance man; a man of many talents who valued freedom and the entrepreneurial spirit. Benjamin Franklin was indeed the "First American."

7. GRIT of Murphy

Courage and resolve; strength of character.

"The way I see it, if you're scared of something, you'd better get busy and do something about it. I'd call that a challenge—and I believe that the way to grow is to meet all the challenges as they come along."- Audie Murphy

Colmar Pocket, France 1945

Feed, chamber, lock, FIRE, unlock, extract, eject, cock. Feed, chamber, lock, FIRE, unlock, extract, eject, cock. Feed, chamber, lock, FIRE. The .50 caliber machine gun violently cycled rounds through its steaming-hot barrel. Audie Murphy gritted his teeth as he fought to control the weapon's bone-jarring recoil. Tracer rounds zipped past him and plinked off the thin armor surrounding his perch on the burning M10 tank destroyer.

"GO!" Audie yelled over his shoulder between bursts of his machine gun. "Move it Sergeant Rayce, get the wounded back into the wood line. I'll provide covering fire while you and the company pull back." He aimed the front sight of his barrel three feet off the ground and engaged the assaulting Germans with grazing fire, cutting many of them right down at the knees.

"Regroup and get the men ready to counter-attack." Audie ducked low as an explosion ripped apart a tree limb just above his head.

"What about you, Lieutenant? We ain't just gonna leave you here." Rayce was already moving back, carrying one of the wounded over his shoulder. "Come on Audie, let's go, pal. You don't gotta do this."

Audie spared a glance down at his friend, Rayce, and the soldier hanging limply over his shoulder. His blood was already starting to drip down onto the French soil. Reluctantly, Audie's hazel eyes then moved over to Beau. He, Rayce, and Beau had been together since Sicily. When they realized they were all from Texas they had become fast friends. That was before the battlefield commission and Audie suddenly finding himself as their commander.

Their friendship continued despite his change in rank. Beau had also grown up as a sharecropper and was twice his size, which wasn't saying too much because, at 5' 5" tall and 115 pounds, Audie wasn't exactly a giant. He also related to Rayce because he, too, came from a big family, though not quite as big as his. Audie was the seventh of twelve while Rayce was only the oldest of nine.

Turned out, all three of them had difficulty getting into the Army when they wanted to enlist after Pearl Harbor. Audie had been turned away by the Army, Navy, and Marines on account of his size. For Beau and Rayce it was age.

Eventually, the Army relented and gave him a shot. They wanted to give him some penny-**ante** job as a cook or something, but Audie wouldn't have that—infantry all the way. He had wanted to be a soldier his entire life.

One of his few memories of his father, before he went and disappeared, was him saying that if he could go back and do it all again, he would be a soldier or a cowboy. Well, there weren't too many opportunities to be a cowboy these days, but there was definitely a need for soldiers and Audie had found his calling.

ANOTHER ROUND RICOCHETED off the turret. Audie returned fire toward the busted old building. Just moments before, two Germans had exited that house, about 100 yards away, and appeared to surrender. Beau had lowered his rifle to accept their surrender when those same Germans had suddenly raised their weapons and cut him down.

His best friend now lay crumpled on the ground just a few meters away. His eyes, still wide with surprise, were now lifeless.

"No, go Rayce. Get the men back and find some cover. We will figure this out in a bit." Audie returned his attention to the machine gun in earnest.

"Please! I can't lose you, too, Audie. Let's go." Rayce could see the rest of the company was almost to the relative safety of the tree line. "Please, Audie."

Adrenaline coursed through Audie's veins and he barely heard the plea of his friend. "Move it, Rayce, that's an ORDER. Get your tail back there and regroup."

He continued firing bursts from the .50 Caliber. The image of Beau collapsing flashing through his mind over and over again. "If I'm not back within the hour, you call brigade and request the reserve. We are not losing this ground." Audie's anger burned brighter at the thought of losing the very ground his friends had died to gain. "We are NOT giving this up."

Reluctantly, Rayce started hustling toward the woods, bullets stitching the ground all around him. He could see the rest of the company crouching behind thick tree trunks, reloading rifles and bandaging wounds. How long would it take to reorganize and muster a viable counter-attack? Everyone was scattered and leaderless. They desperately needed time. Rayce felt a bitter-sweet realization. If anybody could hold off the Germans and give them time; it was Audie. He could probably hold off the whole German army if he had enough bullets.

Rayce knew there was something different about Audie. Something made him scrappy, relentless, and unwilling to back down even in the face of severe bodily harm. He remembered back when 3rd Infantry landed in Sicily, he and Audie had been assigned as division runners. On one of their first scouting patrols, an Italian squad had ambushed them near Canicattì. Audie didn't dive for the ground and hide like everyone else. Instead, he bounded forward to a tree, aimed his rifle and killed two Italian officers.

The patrol sang his praises, but Audie found no joy in shedding his first blood. He felt no qualms, no pride, no remorse. He was just filled with a weary indifference that seemed to follow him. Rayce had asked what made him so brave. He replied simply, "*I'll tell you what bravery really is. Bravery is just determination to do a job that you know has to be done.*"

That made some sense to Rayce. One night, trying to catch some sleep in an abandoned pizzeria, Audie told him about how, starting in the fifth grade, he had to pick cotton for a dollar a day to help his mom feed the family. He shared how much he appreciated his mom. How she had the most beautiful hair he had ever seen; his voice choked up when he revealed that she died when he was only sixteen. Audie said she tried to bring him up right, that she taught him life was sacred.

Since childhood, Audie was acquainted with pain and responsibility. Rayce knew that rough upbringing had forged his friend into something more than a regular soldier. He had an unquenchable fire in his bones to fight for right that drove him to action. If anyone could buy them time, it was Audie.

A GROUP OF FOUR MORE Germans leaped forward from behind a **defilade**, firing their Mauser rifles as they ran. Audie caught their movement out of the corner of his eye and wheeled the machine gun over. His thumbs depressed the butterfly trigger and .50 caliber bullets ripped apart chunks of earth and then flesh as he raked their path. All four Germans fell.

Then, from his blind side, another group of soldiers bounded forward, this time supported by a Panzer tank that recently joined the fray. Audie redirected his fire onto the tank. Its commander was foolish to remain outside of his hatch. Bullets immediately pierced his chest, but not before one of its machine guns scored multiple hits on Audie's tank destroyer.

"Aargh, not again." Audie released the trigger and gripped his thigh. Besides ricochets peppering his face and arms with shards of metal, one of the bullets had drilled deep into his leg. It was the same leg where he'd sustained a shrapnel injury just a few weeks before.

"Rayce is gonna be calling me a gimp again, I just know it." He didn't have time to properly dress the wound. He grabbed a nearby rag, wadded it up, and wedged it between his leg and the turret's wall. "A bit of pressure should keep that bleeding under control." Audie winced as he pressed his leg into the rag.

Pain seared through him, igniting him with even more savage energy.

"At least it ain't Malaria," he assured himself.

He could still remember the fever, tiredness, vomiting, and headaches he had endured in Naples. A simple mosquito bite had caused him the most misery he had ever endured. The doctors said he was one of the lucky ones, many soldiers were so bad they had yellow skin and seizures. Others slipped into comas. Many died. But lying there racked with fever, that last group seemed like the lucky ones.

Nearly an hour had passed. Empty .50 caliber casings surrounded his feet in deep piles. No more belts of ammunition remained. He had used up all the ammunition in his M1 carbine and a Thompson submachine gun he'd found in the turret. He had thrown all of his grenades. Even his pistol was empty. The fire in the tank destroyer was too hot to endure any longer, his hands and face were already red with burns. That was it, he had to abandon the position.

B company was waiting for him in the woods, as long as his leg could hold his weight, he would get to them and lead a counter-attack. He didn't know how many Germans had fallen under his fire; he had lost track after around fifty. What did it matter? There were more Germans out there and he was out of bullets.

Rayce would have the company ready for a scrap by now, and he needed to be there to lead them. After all, he was the company commander, and commanders lead from the front.

WOUNDED AND OUT OF ammunition, Lieutenant Audie Murphy led a successful counterattack. Together they repelled the rest of the Germans and won the day. He went on to receive every military combat award for valor available in the U.S. Army and became the most decorated American combat soldier of World War II. He admitted, "*I was scared before every battle. That old instinct of self-preservation is a pretty basic thing, but while the action was going on some part of my mind shut off and my training and discipline took over. I did what I had to do.*"

Grit defined Audie Murphy's life. He was the consummate underdog who rose up to face and overcome **insurmountable** odds. His life was defined by difficulty, he had ample reason to lie down and quit, yet he never would. Grit enabled this American warrior to demonstrate just how far the bounds of courage can extend.

8. HUMILITY of Aurelius

Modest opinion of one's own importance
& abilities.

H

"The first rule is to keep an untroubled spirit. The second is to look things in the face and know them for what they are." -Marcus Aurelius

Near the Danube River, Europe 175 AD

SUNLIGHT BROKE THROUGH the billowing clouds and reflected off the *lorica segmentata* scale armor of the Roman Legionnaires. Gathered in ordered rows, each soldier looked to his Centurion commander as they formed their lines. Each one made final adjustments to helmet and armor, then kneeled, javelin and shield in hand. A fidgeting tension broiled subtly throughout the formation, a mixture of anticipation and fear.

Emperor Marcus Aurelius rode forward. His sleek white steed's head held high, sure of its steps. Caesar's helmet and breastplate shone bright, though streaked from recent rain. Flanking him were the steely-eyed members of his elite Praetorian Guard. The emperor's presence infused confidence into the men as he approached.

Without prompting, one-by-one, when Caesar passed each Roman soldier stood and brought his fist to his chest exclaiming, "INTEGRITIS." The emperor met their eyes as he passed, nodding to each centurion. "Integritis" was not a greeting, it was a report.

It meant that their armor was oiled and ready, that no rust corrupted the edges of their gladius swords, and that their shields were without flaw. More than that though, the greeting meant that they were ready for battle, ready to become one with their legion—with the empire as a whole. The legion was only as strong as its weakest shield. Each soldier knew his place and committed to Caesar his allegiance.

After trooping the lines, Emperor Aurelius rode to the front of his formations. "Romans, lend me your ears." The voice carried to attentive listeners. "For 200 years Pax Romana has enjoyed peace and prosperity. Our citizens live with order, stability, and the rule of law. But danger has always lurked beyond our borders." He pointed East.

"Last year, Ballomar's forces invaded our land and slew 20,000 of our soldiers—our brothers—at the battle of Carnuntum. Over 900,000 barbarians have ravaged our lands, burned our fields and slaughtered our families ever since. Blood now stains the roads in every direction."

With a calloused hand, he drew his sword; "We gather here for one purpose. To FIGHT. To purge ourselves of this barbarian filth. No Marcomanni, Quadi, or Naristi tribesman will ever step foot on Roman soil again. Today, we fight to preserve our land, our families, our very freedom."

The warrior-emperor held the sword easily in his hand. He squeezed its hilt and felt blood rush into his tightened grip. "*What we do now echoes in eternity.* The barbarians outnumber us by many, but remember one thing..."

A growing rumble rose from the hills to their Front. Caesar could sense his enemy's approach. "Remember this*, death smiles at us all.*" He turned his horse toward the rising cloud of dust and shouted over his shoulder, "*all a man can do is smile back.*"

HIS LEGIONNAIRES UNLEASHED a roar of cheers as they raised their javelins overhead. Calmly, the emperor maintained his position, eyeing the incoming forces.

Roman cavalry crested the hill, pursued by a mixture of mounted and dismounted barbarian infantry. The cavalry had been out front, attempting to identify Ballomar's main body of forces. It appeared to have succeeded.

Captain Gideon of the Praetorian, his longer spatha cavalry sword already red with blood, rode forward to meet his emperor. "Caesar, I bear ill news." His horse reared to a stop next to the emperor. "Ballomar's forces are many, and he is coming straight for us as expected. The trouble is, our outriders identified yet another army of Quadi advancing from the south. Its numbers exceed even that of Ballomar."

"Understood, Gideon. Send your fastest riders to the Danubian fleet, prepare our reserve legions to march and **bolster** this position." The emperor then turned to his generals, "prepare scorpio catapults and ballista crossbows. We must reduce their numbers before they hit our shield wall. Have every archer ready."

The Barbarian hordes were closing in, what was once a rumble in the distance was now a flowing wave of incoming axes, shields, swords, and spears. The Roman troops had heard stories about Carnuntum, stories of barbarians that could smash through shield, helmet, and armor in a single blow. No soldier underestimated this adversary.

Roman archers loosed volley after volley of flaming arrows at the incoming enemy even as the scorpios and ballistas fulfilled their deadly purpose. Still, the masses of incoming barbarians seemed to absorb the losses without losing any momentum. If anything, it only further enraged the attacking **berserkers**.

The lead Barbarian elements crashed pell-mell into the organized Roman shield wall with tidal wave force. For an instant it looked like their overlapping shields would collapse under the unbearable weight of the onslaught, but the endless hours of drill and training held true and the wall regained its footing, then held.

For now.

OUTNUMBERED AND POSSIBLY outmaneuvered, the emperor knew the situation was dire. Desperation started to well up within him, but then he remembered, *you have power over your mind - not outside events.*

He realized this and found strength. He was humble enough to know he did not have all the answers so he called to his trusted Praetorian, "Gideon, you've seen the whole of Ballomar's forces, what say you? How do we prevail this day?"

Gideon pondered a moment, honored by the chance to counsel with Caesar, "We must destroy Ballomar's force before the Quadi attack. We cannot face both Armies at once, we must ensure they remain divided."

"We have no legions to spare. How can we prevent their union?" asked the emperor.

"Sire, you rule over a sprawling empire, Rome has exhausted itself building an extensive system of roads to facilitate trade, communication, and the movement of troops. The Quadi are using those very roads to reach us. Rome also built aqueducts to carry water overland to cities and farms." Gideon leaned toward his commander and gestured with his hand.

"The Quadi must cross the Bavarian gorge during their march. If we can flood the roads and fields with the aqueducts and destroy the bridge, we will halt them in their tracks. We will face but one innumerable barbarian Army, perhaps have an easy day." Gideon leaned back in his saddle.

The emperor had little time to contemplate the course of action. Ballomar's forces were spreading around the shield wall, attempting to wrap itself around the infantry and envelop the artillery positions in their rear.

"Agreed. See to it Gideon, take whoever you need. Ride hard and get the job done. We will continue the fight here." Caesar nodded to his captain.

"Sir, I cannot depart. I will not leave you here to die without my sword to protect you." Gideon protested.

The emperor looked fondly at the young Praetorian. He knew Gideon took his role seriously as one of the emperor's personal bodyguards. He was one of the few elites selected to the post.

A Praetorian had to be in excellent physical condition, have good moral character, and come from a respectable family. Above all, he had to be a formidable warrior. Gideon had all such qualities in abundance.

"*The soul becomes dyed with the color of its thoughts,* captain. So, I recommend you discard any idea of defeat and get moving. Your mission will ensure our success here on this field." The emperor raised his fist to his chest, "Integritis, captain."

Gideon's eyes filled with determination as he rendered the same gesture, "Integritis, sire." He wheeled his horse around and was off in a gallop—driven by grave purpose.

Thirteen legions, each legion filled with seventy-five centuries, each century filled with eighty soldiers, each century led by a grizzled, veteran centurion. Caesar's legions represented the finest trained, equipped, and led professional army the world had ever known. But unless Gideon managed to flood the Bavarian gorge, it would come down to simple arithmetic.

It would be less than 80,000 against hundreds upon hundreds of thousands.

IN WHAT WOULD LATER be memorialized as an act of the gods, the heavens helped Gideon in his quest and opened a torrent of rain that did not relent the rest of the day and into the night. The aqueducts and rivers flooded past their banks and the gorge became an impassable obstacle for the Quadi hordes. The Roman shield wall held and then Roman cavalry drove a wedge through the Barbarian's center and divided their forces.

The work of death continued well into the night, but in the end, Rome's legions emerged victorious. Marcus Aurelias was a philosopher, statesman, and warrior. He reigned over Rome at its **zenith**.

Over a third of the world's population and most of the known earth fell within his empire, he had access to unimaginable luxuries and could have easily delighted in pleasures of the flesh. Instead, he **eschewed** such things and preferred a life of humility. He taught, *"Everything we hear is an opinion, not a fact. Everything we see is a perspective, not the truth."*

"When you arise in the morning, think of what a precious privilege it is to be alive - to breathe, to think, to enjoy, to love."

"He who lives in harmony with himself lives in harmony with the universe."

"The happiness of your life depends upon the quality of your thoughts."

"If it is not right do not do it; if it is not true do not say it."

"The impediment to action advances action. What stands in the way becomes the way. The obstacle is the way."

Humility helped Marcus Aurelias to seek counsel from his generals, to avoid the **narcissistic** trap of believing he had all the answers. He acknowledged that he was mortal, flawed and weak, yet full of potential and capable of great strength. The most powerful man on earth chose humility.

9. INTEGRITY of Regulus

Abiding by strong moral principles; state of being whole.

I

"Your word is your bond." – Unknown

Rome, Italy 255 B.C.

"No, Papa, you can't go. Stay with us. Stay with ME, Papa." His young daughter—Journey—grabbed his hand and looked up with longing. "Why, do you want to leave us? You only just got here, Papa." Tears welled up in her deep blue eyes.

General Marcus Atilius Regulus was standing atop the cold, gray steps outside The Roman Forum. He squeezed his daughter's hand and then lifted her into a warm embrace. "Let us not think of departures, dear."

He turned her in his arms so that she faced outward, the **resplendent** vista of Rome sprawling before them. "Just look at that Journey. Can you believe it? Is it not a marvel that man could build such a city? Even now, the city continues to grow, see there?" Regulus pointed to the rising limestone pillars of the Colosseum, even at this distance, the structure was imposing.

"When complete, that amphitheater will hold over 50,000 spectators. Can you imagine such a number?" Journey nodded in awe, her curly hair waving in the breeze. "Look there as well, that is the Pantheon. The architects say, when they finish, its unreinforced concrete dome will forever be the world's largest."

"Do you know why I admire these structures? Do you know what makes Rome special?" Regulus sat with his daughter; he still had a few precious moments before he would enter the forum.

Journey tapped her chin in contemplation, "Um, are you talking about Romulus and Remus, the twins who founded the city? Is Rome special because they were raised by a she-wolf? I know that story."

Regulus smiled at his daughter's innocence. "No, young one, that is not what makes Rome special, though that legend does unite us. That building, even Rome itself, is special because it is built upon a sure foundation. Rome was not built in a day; it was not even built in one lifetime. Rome is special because those who started building it did so knowing they would not see its completion. The work would pass on to their children and their children's children."

Dramatically, he pounded a fist onto the limestone slab. "Sturdy foundations, Journey." She giggled at her father's theatricality.

"Sturdy foundations support the Forum, the Colosseum, the Pantheon, even our home. With a sure foundation, a building will not fall, but stand tall for **millennia**."

They both looked up at the Forum Romanum, "The same is true of our republic. Rome represents the political, legal, religious, and economic center of our entire civilization. It is built on the principals integritis, dignitas, pietas, and gravitas, remember what that means?"

"I think so, Papa. Isn't it integrity, dignity, devotion, and...wait, I'll remember." She scrunched her nose as she searched her memory. "Oh yes, duty."

She was proud that she remembered the lessons he'd taught her since she was young. "I remember what duty and devotion mean, but I forgot the other two."

He squeezed her to him, "Indeed, you named our foundational ideals. Dignity is your personal character and reputation. It is important that you never do anything that would shame your sweet mother. Would you remember that for me, Journey?" She nodded solemnly.

"Integrity, that is the most important of them all. For it is integrity that binds all other ideals together. It is living true to your principles, fulfilling your promises. It is choosing the harder right over the easier wrong and never being content with a half-truth when the whole can be won. That is the foundation of our civilization's character, of each individual's legacy." Regulus stood; his time had come.

"It is my integrity that demands my departure, sweet Journey. All the gods know that I want nothing more in the world than to remain here with you, your brothers, and your beautiful mother. But, I gave my word to the Carthaginians that I would return and my **parole** has come to an end."

He bent over and kissed her forehead. "I must go speak to the Senate now, wait for me here with your mother, I will come back to you before I depart." Marcia—his wife—slid over and wrapped her arms about Journey's shoulders.

Flanked by legionnaires, two tribunes approached, their togas flowing around them as they walked. "Consul General, the senate is prepared to hear your testimony. Please follow us."

Regulus nodded at his wife, and started walking in their direction. Journey leapt from her seat and had grabbed his waist.

"No, I don't care about integrity or promises; I only care about you, Papa."

He crouched and met her gaze, "I understand how you feel. I love you more than anything, but we must have the courage to do what is right, regardless of the consequences or pain."

THE FORUM WAS OVERFLOWING with senators eager to hear the words of their Consul. The story of Regulus defied belief, it seemed everyone wanted to hear his tale. None remembered a time with more senators, consuls, praetors, and tribunes in one place.

Regulus commanded Rome's forces during the Punic war. His navy defeated the Carthaginians a year before in a battle off Mount Ednomus, in Sicily. His army landed in Africa and led successful campaigns against his enemies. It seemed he was destined for ultimate victory, but in an unexpected twist of fate, a Carthaginian Army was able to overcome Regulus's legions in Tunis and he was taken captive.

Wounded from battle and mourning the loss of his men, Regulus suffered in a Carthaginian cell. After a while, representatives from Carthage approached Regulus with a proposition. They would release Regulus on parole and facilitate his voyage back to his homeland—with two conditions.

First, he must address the Roman Forum and negotiate a peace on behalf of Carthage.

Second, after the negotiations, he would place his affairs in order and return to them within the year.

His captors had assured him that it was entirely within their power to end his life right then and there. They were extending this opportunity to him because they grew weary of war, even though they could destroy Rome itself if needed.

Regulus had asked what they thought would keep him from simply fleeing entirely and never returning to the dank darkness of a prison cell.

"Your integrity." The simple answer was as true as it was painful. "Once you give us your word, General, we will release you on this parole without worry. For you are a man of Rome and we know your word is your bond."

They were right.

For Regulus, there were only two options. He could remain in his cell, watch his wounds fester, and eventually die of malnourishment. Or, he could accept this deal and return to Rome, even if only for a short season. The thought of his family, of Marcia, of his sons and daughter—young Journey—wrenched his heart and he knew he would accept.

"You have my word," Regulus told his captors with quiet dignity.

"I will return to Rome. I will speak of negotiations with the Senate. I will see my family and then return. Realize, I, nor any one man commands the senate. They will decide what they will decide. I can give you no guarantee of peace." His candor impressed the representatives and they agreed.

During his travels through Carthage, on his way to Rome, he noted that the war was taking its toll. The people were weary and their resources strained. To Regulus, it appeared that Carthage was on the brink of collapse. He realized that his captors were using him as a ploy to negotiate a more favorable peace, rather than risk unconditional surrender.

THE REGAL SENATOR LOOKED down on Regulus and asked quizzically, "You mean to say, General, that you are here to sue for peace on behalf of the Carthaginians, but that you, personally, recommend we press the fight? You say Rome will win this war, and that Carthage is ready to fall, that we should not negotiate?"

Regulus looked around the room, "Indeed, that is my recommendation. I've told you what I saw. I will not lie on behalf of Carthage. If I had seen otherwise, my recommendation would be different."

Another senator stood, "Is it not true that you agreed to return to Carthage after your parole?"

"Yes, that was a condition of this parole from the start. I will return of my own accord."

With some bewilderment, the senator asked, "Would not this recommendation all but guarantee an unwelcome return for you in Carthage? You must realize that you are sealing your fate. They will reap vengeance upon you with torture and pain."

The senator continued, "Perhaps you could consider another option. You are familiar with Carthage, you know their lands, their tactics, and their leaders. Regulus, take command yet again, lead our legions into battle, and defeat this foe. None will know of your supposed parole by war's end."

The offer appealed to him. It appealed to his innate desire for personal safety, and of course, he wanted to be with his family. Everything in him yearned to accept. Through that fiery emotion, a still small voice pierced his soul and spoke a single word.

"Integritis."

"I am honored, Senators." Regulus bowed and began walking to the door. "Yet, I cannot accept. I have given my word and it is time for me to say farewell to my family."

HE EXITED THE FORUM and Rome's afternoon sun cast long shadows over the cobblestones. His wife and children were waiting for him, standing next to the chariot that would carry him to the port and the awaiting Carthaginian **envoy**.

Tears filled their eyes. Regulus knew his family was trying so hard to be strong. "I love you. You will all be in my thoughts from when I rise till I lay to rest. My thoughts will be of you." He hugged each one, starting with his loyal wife and working his way from oldest to youngest. Finally, he came to his youngest, his daughter.

"You know I love you, don't you, Journey?" He squeezed her tight. She couldn't reply, emotion choked the words in her throat. "I will always love you. My love for you is bigger than the colosseum, bigger than Rome." He kissed her forehead for the final time.

He set her down and mounted the chariot. His tears blurred his vision as he looked back at his family. The horses stirred, ready to set off. Journey suddenly burst out of her mother's arms and raced to the chariot.

"WAIT, wait, please wait!" She was sobbing, her voice desperate. Regulus touched his driver's shoulder, staying his hand. He stepped to his daughter.

"I will miss you, Daddy. I will miss you so, so much." She squeezed him as tight as her trembling little body possibly could.

"My sweet girl, I will miss you too. More than you can know."

REGULUS RETURNED TO Carthage. He gave an honest accounting of his time before the senate. The Carthaginians were enraged; they stripped him of his robes and cast him back into prison. The Punic War continued, with each loss his captors dragged Regulus from his cell to endure unimaginable torture.

Eventually, Regulus succumbed to injury and perished, his body battered and broken. Nevertheless, his integrity, his honor, and the foundation of his personal legacy remained entirely intact.

"When you are able to maintain your own highest standards of integrity—regardless of what others may do—you are destined for greatness." - Napoleon Hill

"Integrity is doing the right thing when no one is watching." - CS Lewis

"One of the truest tests of integrity is blunt refusal to be compromised." – Chinua Achebe

*"Men of integrity, by their very existence, rekindle the belief that as a people we can live above the level of moral **squalor**. We need that belief; a cynical community is a corrupt community."* -John Gardner

"Integrity is fundamental to being men, integrity means being truthful, but it also means accepting responsibility and honoring commitments and covenants." -D. Todd Christofferson

"You are what you do, not what you say you'll do." -Carl Jung

Integrity motivated Regulus's actions. He could have escaped into the country and never returned to Carthage. He could have enjoyed the company of his children and friends. He could have avoided immense physical torment. But, for Regulus, his word truly was his bond.

10. JUSTICE of Crazy Horse

The condition of being morally correct or fair.

"Upon suffering beyond suffering, the Red Nation shall rise again, and it shall be a blessing for a sick world. A world filled with broken promises, selfishness, and separations. The world longs for light again."- Crazy Horse

Little Big Horn River, Montana Territory 1876

The cavalrymen formed a hasty perimeter and prepared for the next attack. Desperate, they had to resort to shooting their horses and using their lifeless flesh for protection from endlessly incoming arrows, bullets, and blades on an endless prairie with no hope of cover. Bodies littered the grassy field in every direction, white and red man alike. In the center of the position, a cavalryman in a buckskin jacket and bright red scarf shouted orders to those remaining.

"Custer." A hundred meters away, atop a painted steed, Crazy Horse muttered the name as he eyed the man stoically.

There he was. He was the one who led the early morning raid at Washita. The one who killed Chief Black Kettle and 103 Cheyenne, including women and children. The white-man called it a battle. He called it a massacre.

It was not the first. It would not be the last.

"Brother, Two Moon just returned with some of our Dog Soldiers, they say that the white man's warriors are trapped down by the river. They make no further effort to reach their war chief. All is going according to plan. Do you wish me to order the final charge?" The Native American brave eyed Crazy Horse intently.

"Has Chief Gall heard this news?" Crazy Horse was a Lakota, a man of action, but he respected the frail nature of his alliance with the rest of the tribes. He had to keep them informed.

The Lakota, Northern Cheyenne, Arapaho, and other Sioux had assembled over 2,000 warriors for this great battle. Success depended on their ability to fight as one. Though they surpassed the white man in numbers, they would never win without a coordinated attack. The Cavalry, with their striped trousers, had weapons that could slay many warriors before they were close enough to use their bows.

"Gatling Gun," that was the name of their newest **fell** instrument. Its rotating barrels spewed dragon's fire and never seemed to reload.

The great spirit smiled upon them this day, for some reason, the yellow-haired Custer did not bring Gatling Guns to this battle. It looked like the cavalry was only using Springfield Trapdoor single-shot rifles, formidable weapons—but no Gatling Guns.

Crazy horse raised his own rifle. The 1876 Winchester lever-action repeater was far superior to the soldiers' Springfields. It was one of Sitting Bull's great achievements. The old chief had happened upon some freelance trappers in the Dakota territory. He discovered their skill went beyond fur trapping; their real money was in arms dealing. Sitting Bull was glad to offer payment if it meant his braves would be equipped with the new lever-action rifles for the upcoming battle.

"Chief Gall knows all, Crazy Horse, he awaits your order." The brave was anxious for the fight.

"Have all the tribes unite on me. Leave only the Cheyenne Dog Soldiers at the river. They will keep the other companies of the white man trapped until this is over. Soon, we will ride forward and cut down what is left of Custer's band. We will offer no surrender, not that it matters, these Soldiers would never accept defeat." Crazy Horse rode off in a gallop, headed to join his massing group of Lakota.

CUSTER'S MEN WERE WORKING in a frenzy. There was no time to waste, men reloaded rifles, redistributed ammunition, and took carefully aimed shots at any braves that came within range. Their horse carcass barricade would prove useful enough. Without cover they would be slain in an instant, their horses' last act of service was to give them a fighting chance.

Still, Custer's heart broke when he had to put down Vic. He couldn't bear to look him in the eyes as he pulled the trigger. Now his powerful thoroughbred was lying dead at his feet. Kneeling behind his fallen steed, he felt bitter irony as he thought of Vic's full name.

"Victory."

Maybe not today, old friend, but maybe there is a sort of victory in a warrior's death.

"What are we gonna do Georgie? We ain't got enough bullets left to plug even a fraction of them Indians. Look at 'em, there must be thousands. What are they waiting for? Why don't they just come and finish the job?" His brother, Thomas, squinted down his barrel as he spoke.

"It's like our own little Thermopylae here, except we ain't fighting no dadgum Persians." Six years his junior, there was always room for a joke from his kid brother.

Custer felt pride in Thomas, in all his men. They were fighters, every single one. Sure, they called him "*Iron Butt*" behind his back, but that was because of his physical stamina in the saddle and his strict discipline. That very discipline had kept them alive so far.

It was that same discipline that had given him victory over J.E.B. Stuart at Gettysburg and Jubal Early at Cedar Creek. If Major Reno were able to fight through to his position, they might have a chance. They might be low on bullets, but courage they had in spades.

His younger brother, Thomas, crouching right next to him, had twice been awarded the medal of honor during the civil war. He had been with him from the start. Custer had promised their mother that he would look after him. He hoped to make good on that promise.

"The battle ain't over yet. Captain Benteen has three companies of troopers who know to ride toward the sound of the guns. Our cavalry might just arrive and turn the tide. Till then, we are going to hold this here hill. I fancy this spot; it has a pretty view." He nudged his brother with his elbow and gave him a wink.

Though there was still plenty of fight left in his soldiers, he could sense the dread building among them. The number of braves joining the already formidable host that encircled their position was not promising. The men had heard the stories, scalping and mutilation of captured troopers.

No, surrender was absolutely not an option.

"Thousands," was what his scout had told him. Now that estimate felt like an understatement. At the center of the growing line of painted braves, Custer's eyes came to a warrior painted with lightning bolts across his cheeks and a look of cold determination.

It was Crazy Horse.

EVERY WARRIOR WAS GATHERED. The time had come. Many of the braves beside him were veterans of the Black Hills War. Some were young, tasting battle for the first time. Others were old, far too old for a seasonal hunt, but determined to participate in this fight. Some carried tomahawks, others Winchesters, some used rusted muzzle-loading rifles, they were a **hodge-podge** of tribes, equipment, and personalities.

Despite the disparity, at this moment they were all one in purpose, and that purpose was justice.

They demanded justice for the women and children murdered at Washita. They demanded justice for the 4,000 plus Cherokee who died along the Trail of Tears during the white president Andrew Jackson's Indian Removal Policy. They demanded justice for the broken promises, lies, and deceit that the white man continually forced upon them.

No more.

His people would not remove themselves to one of their reservations, confined in squalor. They would fight for their freedom, fight for their customs and mores. They would not give up and live idly, escaping their woes in drunken stupor brought on by the firewater the white man loved to offer.

No, this day they would fight, and lady justice would receive her payment in blood.

Crazy Horse reared his charger high and unleashed a battle cry. The aloofness, shyness, and lonesomeness so often associated with him instantly vanished, replaced by an infectious audacity.

He remembered his vision from the Black Hills and the promise that as long as he dressed modestly and did not take any scalps or war trophies, then he would not be harmed in battle. This was his moment.

"Hokahey! Today is a good day to die." His yell inspired cries from all sides and it spread in a wave, filling the valley with the sound of war. He charged forward with his eyes locked on the Cavalryman in a buckskin jacket and blonde curly hair.

Custer was his.

As the braves initiated their charge, Custer leapt to his feet *"Hurrah boys, we've got them! We'll finish 'em up and then get on home to our station."* He gave his final effort to inspire his men as he fired round after round from his Colt Peacemaker Revolver.

When the sun set that day, 268 cavalrymen lay dead upon the field, each one fought to the very end. As the braves worked their way through the killing field, they found Custer's body lying next to his brother.

They had perished together, back to back, united—even in death.

CRAZY HORSE'S ACTIONS during the Little Big Horn inspired awe among the tribes. Many spoke of how he rode closest to the soldiers, and even with all the soldiers shooting at him, he was never hit.

He lived through the war and once said, *"We did not ask you white men to come here. The Great Spirit gave us this country as a home. You had yours. We did not interfere with you. We do not want your civilization!"*

"A very great vision is needed, and the man who has it must follow it as the eagle seeks the deepest blue of the sky."

"They say we massacred him, but he would have done the same to us had we not defended ourselves and fought to the last."

"We do not inherit the land from our ancestors. We borrow it from our children."

Justice drove the Sioux nation to unite in defense of their lands. The U.S. government compromised its integrity too many times as it dealt with America's **indigenous** population. Crazy Horse dedicated his life to protecting his people and the pursuit of an ideal that should not have been so **elusive**—justice.

11. KNOWLEDGE of Carson

Understanding obtained by experience or study.

"There is a tendency of people to try to make you believe only a few people are smart. As a brain surgeon, I know better than that." – Ben Carson

Detroit, Michigan 1969

"Go to your room, right now, mister." His mom, Sonya, had a face red with anger.

"Why? Going to my room ain't gonna solve nothing. I am sick of this, Mom. You trying to run a **dictatorship** in this house." Ben was just as mad as his mom, and he was not going to take it anymore.

"You meant to say 'going to your room will not solve anything.' If you are going to sass me, then have the self-respect to use proper grammar." She crossed her arms and set her jaw. If this was going to turn into a battle, she was ready to hold her ground.

"You want to talk then? So, talk."

Ben looked at her with contempt. "I don't even know where to start. I mean it, you are a dictator. Hitler, Franco, Salazar, Mussolini, all those fascists they talk about in history class, you know those guys? You're worse. They may have censored the newspapers but they didn't control their peoples' every action." He raised his hands in exasperation.

"Outside of school, homework, chores and everything going on in my life, you demand that I read books and write not one, but TWO book reports every single week. On top of that, you won't even let me catch my breath and watch some television. I am a teenager mom; teenagers watch television. I don't even understand half of the jokes at school because I am **oblivious** to their references," embarrassment flooded his memory.

"I'm out there looking like a fool, every single day." He was about to continue but his mom raised a finger.

"Just one second, do you really want to compare me to Hitler? You do remember that your father fought in World War II. He spent years over in Europe, he saw what happened over there. Death camps, gas chambers, mass graves, millions upon millions dead." She paused to let that sink in.

"He wouldn't even talk about some of the things he saw." His mother shook her head in disbelief.

She continued, "Do you think you have it as bad as the Jews who were rounded up and herded like cattle into train cars, stripped of all their possessions, even their families. How do you think your father would feel about this thoughtless comparison?"

Ben turned away from his mom and leaned against the window, Detroit's city street just beyond the windowpane. He looked at the smoke billowing from a nearby smokestack.

An image flashed into his mind of a huddled group of emaciated figures in striped pajamas getting pushed into what was supposed to be a shower, then poison gas pouring from the shower heads instead. He had eavesdropped on the conversation years ago and heard his dad's voice tremble as he spoke.

"I have no idea how dad would feel about anything. He is gone. He isn't coming back." His head lowered, a sense of defeat sweeping over him.

Then, sincerely, he asked, "Why did he leave mom. One day he was telling me about how he saw Audie Murphy take on a whole German company by himself, the next day he was gone. Why?"

Then, painfully, he looked up at his mom. He didn't really want to say it, but he was so mad, his insides were burning him up. He couldn't let her get away with ruling over him like this. She needed to come off her high horse and stop pretending like her impossible demands and constant supervision was tough love. She was a tyrant and he was powerless to change things.

He could at least make the tyrant bleed.

"It was because of you, wasn't it? You drove him away. It's not that he didn't love me, he just hated you so much he couldn't take it anymore and he abandoned us. Was that it? Was it?"

His mom did not respond. She just stood there looking at him, tears starting to well in her eyes. A full minute passed. Then, slowly, she turned and walked to the couch. She sat down and looked over at him with a seriousness he had not expected.

"DO YOU HONESTLY WANT to know why your father left?"

She said it so calmly. There was not a hint of anger; the heat of their argument was suddenly gone. Ben had not seen his mom like this before. She was different; the tyrant was suddenly gone. Someone new was before him.

For the first time, his mother—the determined single-parent, working mom—was vulnerable.

"There is a reason I rarely speak of your father, Ben. There are things that I have kept from you because I did not want to ruin what memories you have of your father."

It was not easy for her to continue. "When we were young, we felt like we could take on the whole world together. He was a Baptist minister and it seemed like he had a scripture to handle any situation."

She smiled to herself, "Not just the reference, mind you. He had the scriptures memorized, entire passages. I couldn't believe that the man, who just a few years before was shooting machine guns was now a man of God, quoting the bible. Later, he worked at a Cadillac plant. You know he was a very hard worker."

Ben interrupted, "I know all this stuff mom. You aren't telling me anything new."

"He traveled a lot. You were young, but you can probably remember that he was gone, sometimes months at a time. He said the travel was required by Cadillac. They needed him to go check on another plant, so he had to be gone." She interlaced her fingers and leaned forward.

"One time, I decided it would be fun to surprise your father. He had been gone a lot that year. It seemed like he was overextended, trying to support our family. So, I decided that for his next trip I was going to come along to be there to make him meals and help where I could. To make it extra special, I was going to surprise him at his hotel room." Her expression darkened.

"Only, he never went to a hotel room. He drove straight to a small house out in the suburbs. I was following him in a taxi. He must not have noticed. When he got out of his car and walked to the house, he was greeted by a woman and two children. He hadn't even made it to the steps before they ran out to meet him." Tears started to brim over his mom's eyes.

"I thought maybe he was visiting some family, a cousin I hadn't met yet or something. I got out of my taxi and started walking toward them." Ben's mom raised her head and met his gaze.

"That was when I saw him kiss her. It wasn't a peck like they do in Europe to say hello. No, it was a full, romantic, even passionate kiss." Her shoulders were trembling as she relived the memory.

"It suddenly hit me, all of the travel, all of the confusion about finances, all of the random bills, all of the odd stories, the pieces of the puzzle suddenly came together. Your father was living a double life, he wasn't just cheating on me. He had an entirely different family." She paused.

"I tried to run away. I wanted to get back in the taxi and escape, but the woman had seen me. She waved and called me over. I just stood there, looking at all of them. The woman asked your father who I was." The tears were real now, sobs racked his mother, she could barely get the next words out.

"He looked right at me and said he had no idea who I was."

BEN COULD NOT BELIEVE his ears. It wasn't possible. His dad was a war hero, he was a man of God. He would never; he could never do such a thing. Not to his mom, not to the mother of his children. A rush of confusion flowed over him. None of this made sense, none of it.

"Your father never came back from that trip. I didn't dare go up to them, I just left. What was there left for me to do? We divorced shortly thereafter, and you boys and I have been on our own ever since." She smoothed her apron as she spoke.

"You wanted to know. Now you do. Maybe you were right; maybe it was me all along." She looked broken.

In vivid detail, Ben's perspective left behind the selfish view of adolescence suddenly zoomed out. He no longer just saw his personal turmoil.

He could see his whole family. He could see his mom working multiple jobs, struggling to make ends meet. He could see her trying to find food stamps in her purse at the store while others in line waited impatiently. He could see her arriving late in the evening, long after he and his brother were asleep, and her quietly entering the room to kiss him on the forehead.

Ben had no words.

"Can you understand why I do what I do, son? I am doing all I can to ensure you and your brother have a bright future. I have you read books and write those reports because knowledge is power." Her voice gained some confidence.

"The way that you break free from poverty is through knowledge, education, and hard work. I will not have my boys living on food stamps. You are going to rise above this. You are going to be better than your father, better than me."

Compassion sparked in his heart, it burned brighter than his frustration ever could. He flew over to his mom and wrapped her in his arms. Tears of his own suddenly pouring from his eyes.

"I'm sorry, Mom, I'm so sorry." His face was buried in her neck. "I know you are doing the best you can for us; I know this can't be easy. You've been fighting for us all along. You just want us to succeed."

He paused for a moment and then whispered, "I love you, Mom."

DR. BEN CARSON WENT on to college at Yale and then thrived at medical school, choosing the demanding field of neurosurgery. He went on to become a chief of pediatric neurosurgery. He received more than 60 honorary doctorates, wrote over 100 neurosurgical publications, and was selected by the Library of Congress as one of 89 "Living Legends" on its 200th anniversary. When he received the Presidential Medal of Freedom, the highest civilian award in the United States, he said he owed it all to his mother.

He proclaimed that "*through hard work, perseverance and a faith in God, you can live your dreams.*"

"*You have the ability to choose which way you want to go. You have to believe great things are going to happen in your life. Do everything you can - prepare, pray and achieve - to make it happen.*"

"*It doesn't matter if you come from the inner city. People who fail in life are people who find lots of excuses. It's never too late for a person to recognize that they have potential in themselves.*"

"*Success is determined not by whether or not you face obstacles, but by your reaction to them. And if you look at these obstacles as a containing fence, they become your excuse for failure. If you look at them as a hurdle, each one strengthens you for the next.*"

"Happiness doesn't result from what we get, but from what we give."

Knowledge was what Sonya wanted for her children. It was the vehicle that lifted her children out of a desperate situation. Dr. Ben Carson's life is a beacon of hope to all who feel the odds are stacked against them. Knowledge is power.

12. LOYALTY of Crockett

Faithful to a cause, ideal, custom, or institution; allegiance.

"Loyalty to the country always. Loyalty to the govern-ment when it deserves it."– Mark Twain

The Alamo, San Antonio, Texas 1836

Davy Crockett was wounded. A cannonball from one of General Santa Anna's Mexican artillery had shattered it-self into the church's rampart and spewed shrapnel and brick in every direction. Crockett was, unluckily, close enough to be peppered in the forehead and arm by razor-sharp slivers.

Now, aiming his rifle with precision was a tad trickier, on account of the sweat and blood that kept sneaking into his right eye. He wiped it away.

"Doggone Davy, you gonna pull the trigger or what? Them Mexicans are scurrying around out there and you're just point-ing at them. Why don't you give 'em the ol' what for? They just done bloodied ya; so, shoot 'em why don't ya?" Jim Bowie was taking trained shots as he spoke.

"Well, if you would just be patient, Jim, I am trynna pick a good target over here. If you remember, Colonel Travis said we gotta conserve ammunition."

Crockett patted his .40-caliber flintlock rifle affectionately. "'Old Betsy' here ain't gonna be wasting a bullet on no Mexican private like you are over there. Nope, she has her sights set on one of them officers."

"That so?" said Bowie. "Just what makes you so sure you can even tell which ones which at this distance? Travis won't let anyone shoot at them except you, me, and your best Tennesseans, because—like you said—ammunition is scarce."

Reluctantly, he continued. "So, I'll admit you and your men are dropping Mexican soldiers like prairie dogs, but just how can you tell who is an officer?"

"Well, the way I figure it, looks like the Generalissimo has around 2,000 men out there. That's probably a brigade. So, a brigade is made up of what? That's right, battalions. I'm guessing two, each with 1,000 men." Davy deliberately used a **didactic** tone.

"The battalion probably has four or five companies in it, with a couple hundred soldiers per company. A company is led by a captain and has four platoons, each platoon led by a lieutenant. You following me so far, Jim?

Bowie, exasperated, rolled his eyes. "I didn't ask for a dadgum lesson on military structure, did I. Did you think I was a West Point cadet?"

"Well, maybe not, but I'm not gonna let this opportunity to learn something sneak past you, my friend. Out there, out beyond those buildings at 100 meters is what I reckon to be two artillery batteries. So, I'm looking for captains and lieutenants. Each cannon's gotta have at least one. He will probably be waving his arms around giving orders."

Crockett adjusted his coonskin hat and squeezed the trigger. 'Old Betsy' recoiled at the blast. In the distance a lone Mexican officer collapsed. "Like that, right there, that was definitely an officer."

Bowie smiled at his newfound friend, "You claim to be a backwoods frontiersman like me, Davy, but I know better. You are one of them in-tee-lectuals, ain't ya."

"Now them's fighting words, Jim, how dare you." Crockett feigned insult. "Why, if I didn't know about the Sandbar Fight, I would challenge you to a duel right here and now."

THE SANDBAR FIGHT WAS the event that propelled Jim Bowie into the public consciousness. It reached near mythological proportions.

Jim was involved in a duel, that much was clear. During the event, Jim Bowie was shot in the hip and pistol-whipped. While lying on the ground, his opponent approached and then stabbed him in the chest with a cane sword.

When he stepped on Jim's chest to withdraw the blade, Jim grabbed him and with his other hand gutted him with a large knife. He went on to defeat the rest of his attackers before collapsing. It was a miracle he was even alive.

"Nah, don't put too much credit in them tales. Besides, you're the one who is the 'King of the Wild Frontier' ain't ya?" Bowie prodded Crockett as he reloaded.

"Well, like you said, can't put too much stock in tales. If I'm being honest, I didn't kill a bear when I was only three years old." Crockett squeezed the trigger again.

"I was five."

Bowie laughed heartily. "Now that's what I like to hear. Finally, some doggone humility."

Then, a bit more somberly, he said. "Here we are thirteen days into a siege, surrounded, outnumbered, nearly out of ammunition, and the Mexicans have been charging our position since sunup. Odds are nobody is walking away from this place. I gotta ask you something."

They both had to duck as a fresh volley of cannon and rifle fire bombarded the Alamo's walls.

"What might that be, Jim?" Crockett was reloading again.

"Why are you here? Why didn't you just stay up in Washington? I don't want to hear anything about the call of adventure either. I want to know the truth. What drove you to leave that all behind and die with a bunch of Texans?"

Crockett was caught a bit off-guard by the question. It was something that he contemplated often. Normally, he would just say that Texas was the garden spot of the world. The best land and the best prospects for health he ever saw. He said he believed in its fight for freedom, that Texas had a world of country ready to be settled.

But that wasn't the whole story.

IN TRUTH, IT WAS MORE than that. It was his sad realization that even at the height of his influence, Crocket was unable to be the force for good he hoped for in Washington. He had joked to his friends, "*There ain't no ticks like poly-ticks. Bloodsuckers all.*"

President Andrew Jackson's Indian Removal Act was the final straw.

Everyone expected Crockett to bow to the name of Andrew Jackson, even at the expense of his conscience and judgment. Such action was new to him, a total stranger to his principles. His mother taught him to let his tongue speak what his heart thinks, so he was an outspoken opponent to the vile law.

When his own party requested his silence and support for the president he replied, *"I have always supported measures and principles, not men."*

Later, a newspaper asked his opinion and he replied, *"I voted against this Indian bill, and my conscience yet tells me that I gave a good, honest vote, and one that I believe will not make me ashamed in the day of judgment."*

Many of those who supported him did not appreciate his candor. Some financial backers threatened to abandon him. But Crockett always believed, *"better to keep a good conscience with an empty purse, than to get a bad opinion of myself, with a full one."*

Despite Crockett's efforts, Jackson's Indian Removal Act passed. He remembered saying, *"I have suffered myself to be politically sacrificed to save my country from ruin and disgrace and if I am never again elected, I will have the gratification to know that I have done my duty."*

When Crockett found out about Jackson's soldiers forcibly removing thousands of Cherokee and driving them through frigid winter conditions into an unknown land, most dying along the way, he had enough. Crocket packed his things and bid **adieu** to all those politicians in Washington, *"You can all go to hell; I will go to Texas."*

He looked over at Jim and was about to open up about his experience as a Tennessee member of the House of Representatives when instead he just said, "Loyalty. I'm here out of loyalty to the cause of freedom. I had little success helping the native tribes find freedom, I figure I'd give it another shot in Texas."

BUGLES RANG OUT, THE Mexican Infantry was massing for another assault. Crockett did some quick math in his head, of their 250 defenders only a handful were in any condition to fight. Their ammunition was all but gone and their cannons had only a few rounds left.

Crockett eyed Jim's Bowie Knife, "I reckon it'll be time to use that thing again here in a minute."

Bowie pulled out the knife, "This little Arkansas Toothpick?" He spun the huge blade easily in his fingers.

"Yep, I reckon you're right. It's been a pleasure Davy, I'm glad I got to know ya."

"Likewise, Jim." They both then directed their attention to the incoming line of infantry, firing their rifles in unison.

GENERAL SANTA ANNA overwhelmed the small band of fighters and killed every single one of the defenders. All 250 bodies were piled up and burned outside the church. The battle was over and the Mexican flag rose high above the walls.

"Remember the Alamo!"

The exclamation instantly became the battle cry of every Texas soldier. A month later, on April 21, 1836, the Texans defeated the Mexican Army at the Battle of San Jacinto and won their independence.

Davy Crockett left the following remarks, *"Remember these words when I am dead. First, be sure you're right, then go ahead."*

"I'm that same David Crockett, fresh from the backwoods, half-horse, half-alligator, a little touched with the snapping turtle; can wade the Mississippi, leap the Ohio, ride upon a streak of lightning, and slip without a scratch down a honey locust tree."

Loyalty led Davy Crocket to serve his country in Washington and loyalty again led him to fight alongside Jim Bowie in the Alamo. He was faithful to the cause of freedom until the very end.

13. MODERATION of
Rickenbacker

Avoidance of excess or extremes in behavior & opinion.

"Moderation in all things is the best policy." -Plautus

Somewhere in the Central Pacific Ocean, 1942

Twenty-one days. Water lapped over the edges of the life raft. The subtle urge to vomit tickled the back of his throat, simple **apathy** kept him from retching. Throbbing sensations burned behind his temples and eyes.

Wait, maybe it was twenty-four. Yes, that was it, twenty-four days had passed. Blisters covered his parched lips, he mouthed the number, "twenty-four."

Eddie Rickenbacker was 52 years old, he was a two-time medal of honor recipient, a fighter ace, a race car driver, and an entrepreneur. Now he was a castaway, drifting in the ocean with little chance of recovery.

"I can't, I can't, I can't take it anymore." Alex was dehydrated and delirious. "I'm so thirsty, I have to drink something, I have to." He rolled over and crawled to the raft's edge.

"No! Don't do it." Rickenbacker was the oldest on the raft, by a long shot. He had assumed the role of de facto leader and had helped them ration what little resources left to their disposal.

"You can't drink saltwater. Alex, we have gone over this. It will kill you." Rickenbacker reached over and grabbed Alex by the leg and started dragging him away from the raft's edge. "Your cells won't be able to handle the concentration of salt; it'll dehydrate you even further. Listen to me, Alex."

Alex kicked at Rickenbacker wildly, "No, I'm too thirsty; I don't care; I have to drink something." His foot connected with Eddie's face and he lost his grip.

"Please, Alex, don't kill yourself."

It was too late. His words were lost in the ocean breeze. Alex was leaning over the edge lapping up gallons of water like a rabid dog. Then, he was coughing and sputtering.

He collapsed back into the raft, sobs replacing the coughs. "We are all dead anyway."

Eddie slid toward Alex and scooped the boy into his arms. Alex was a crewman of the B-17 that had been flying him and the rest to see Macarthur over in the Philippines. Obviously, they hadn't made it to their destination. A faulty navigational instrument led them hundreds of miles off course.

They simply ran out of fuel.

He would never forget the stark inevitability of it all as he peered into the cockpit. The pilots were milking the engines for every last drop of thrust, but the fuel cells were empty. In every direction, there was nothing but blue water meeting a blue horizon. Ditching was their only option.

ALEX'S BODY FELT SO frail. Everyone in the rafts had lost weight, their bodies essentially **consuming** themselves for weeks now. Alex though, he felt as light as a feather. In the morning sun, his face suddenly looked angelic and young.

So young.

Eddie tried to remember the days when he too was young, when there was more to life than sea and sky. He recalled driving race cars. His friends called him "Fast Eddie." He could see the checkered flag of the Indianapolis 500. Four times, he raced there, four times before the great war.

Great War. The war to end all wars. Boy, had they all been wrong on that.

He believed that men grew only in proportion to the service they rendered to their fellow men and women. There was never a question in his mind if he would volunteer. He grew up in Columbus, Ohio, not far from the very place where the Wright Brothers **prototyped** the first airplane. He was going to be an aviator, no matter what.

He did not have much formal education, but his father had given him a love for engineering and Eddie liked to read. He studied the field of aviation **voraciously**. *"A machine has to have a purpose,"* his father said. Eddie became a master of how airplanes worked and how to maintain them.

After some convincing, the Army admitted him to the "Hat-in-the-Ring" 94th Aero Squadron. He believed that aviation was proof that given the will, humans had the capacity to achieve the impossible. Eddie's prowess in the air earned him multiple victories over German opponents.

A fellow aviator asked how he balanced maneuvering the airplane and shooting. He simply replied, *"The better I shoot, the less I have to maneuver."*

Still, he never made light of what they were doing in the skies above France. After he was promoted to Captain, Eddie felt the weight of command press down on him. The aerial combat was increasingly difficult, the German's new Fokker D. VII airplane was a formidable machine. Germans were saying it could turn a mediocre pilot into a good one and a good pilot into an ace.

They were not wrong.

Some of his pilots were intimidated by the sudden shift in German capability. Eddie assured them, *"I shall never ask any pilot to go on a mission that I won't go on."* He went on to shoot down more than fourteen of the new German biplanes.

Back at the airfield his men congratulated him and cheered his status as the fighter ace with the most kills. Eddie wasn't in the mood to celebrate. He looked at his men somberly and said, *"Fighting in the air is not a sport. It is scientific murder."* He pulled off his cap and walked toward the bunks. He needed his rest, tomorrow there would be more missions to fly.

In the end, he flew more than 300 combat hours and had 26 aerial victories. He flew more than any U.S. pilot and was their most successful fighter ace in the Great War.

That was a lifetime ago. He could hardly recognize the young, bright-eyed face in his memories.

"LISTEN TO ME, ALEX, *I believe that if you think about disaster, you will get it. Brood about death and you hasten your demise. Think positively and masterfully with confidence and faith, and life becomes more secure, more fraught with action, richer in achievement and experience.* If you say you're going to die, you'll be starting down that path."

Alex was whimpering now, his energy completely sapped.

"We are going to make it. I read a quote once; it was from a man named Plutarch. He said, *'Many things which cannot be overcome when they are together yield themselves up when taken little by little.'* Do you understand that? You can do incredibly hard things; you just have to tackle the problem a piece at a time." He caressed the boy's head.

"Take us here in this raft for instance. When we ditched the B-17 we knew we needed to survive out here, so we brought all the provisions we could find onto the raft. With moderation, that food and water lasted almost a week. Then, when the storms billowed, we were able to collect rainwater and ration that for another two weeks." Alex was barely conscious; Eddie was practically talking to himself.

"Remember when that seagull landed on my head? What were the odds of that happening? It was a miracle, but we didn't just consume the whole bird at once. No, with moderation we had food for multiple days and then were able to use some of the flesh as bait to catch fish." Eddie leaned back and squinted up into the sky.

"Surviving at sea for twenty-four days is an impossible task. Yet, here we are. We have taken the task on little by little and made it this far. That is saying something, don't you think, Alex?"

Eddie squeezed Alex's shoulder, "Don't you think buddy? Isn't it amazing we've made it this far?" He felt no response from the boy.

"Alex, come on son, answer me." He was shaking him now. "Alex, ALEX, wake up; you've got to wake up!" The boy's head lolled to the side, the tears left dried streaks across his cheeks.

There was no pulse.

Eddie leaned into the boy's chest and broke down in tears. "No, Alex, you can't do this to me. We were going to all make it together. Why, Alex, why did you leave us?" He rested his head on the boy's chest for what seemed like hours. Part of Eddie started to wonder if Alex had made the better choice.

Then he remembered something he read in another book. It was Plato. *"The man who makes everything that leads to happiness depend upon himself, and not upon other men, has adopted the very best plan for living happily. This is the man of moderation, the man of manly character and of wisdom."*

Rickenbacker sat up in the raft. He reached over and covered Alex's face with a cloth. He stared out over the ocean, until the sun started to sink into the horizon and the blue sky yielded itself to the brilliant orangey blaze of sunset.

An engine hummed in the distance.

He thought it was his imagination, hallucinations finally driving him mad. There it was again though, a distinct buzz of a diesel motor. Others in the raft started sitting up. An airplane suddenly materialized out of the setting sun. It was a U.S. Navy search plane. Their days adrift at sea were finally over.

EDDIE RICKENBACKER survived the war and continued a life of service. He said, *"The biggest lesson I learned is, if you have all the fresh water you want to drink and all the food you want to eat, you ought never to complain about anything."*

"Most of one's troubles in this world come from something inside one's self."

"Every disappointment that came to me brought with it an enduring lesson that repaid me eventually tenfold."

Moderation helped Eddie Rickenbacker survive in that life raft for twenty-four days. He also used moderation as he pursued his passion of racing cars and aviation. He avoided excess and achieved great things. Moderation was his watchword.

14. NOBILITY of Washington

Quality of having high moral qualities or character; royal heritage.

"The harder the conflict, the greater the triumph."
-George Washington

Trenton, American Colonies, 1776

HESSIANS. CRACK MERCENARY troops all the way from Germany. Disciplined veterans from the Napoleonic wars. General George Washington couldn't shake the thought of his very worthy adversary as he rode at the head of his ragtag column of patriots. His horse's hooves sank deep into the mud as it trotted forward.

Sleet and snow continued to fall all around the column, specks of white barely visible in the dark night. The foul weather was as much a blessing as it was a curse. The dark clouds blotted out the moon and stars, covering the earth in a blanket of darkness.

Just a few hours before, Washington, General Ewing, and General Cadwalader had crossed the half-frozen Delaware river. They each crossed with a division of men, around a thousand each—except Washington. His force was the main effort and, thus, weighted with more men. Turbulent water, driving wind, and hail made the possibility of capsizing all too real.

They hoped that the cold, **incessant** sleet would keep Hessian sentinels near their warming fires. Plus, it was Christmas, and Washington was willing to use any ploy he could muster to secure the element of surprise. Even mercenaries wouldn't suspect the colonial militia to move on Christmas.

Still, the weather was taking its toll on the men. It was certainly a curse to his soldiers without shoes. Washington had walked through his camp before night fell and knew full well that he was asking a lot of his troops. Many were walking on bloodied feet, protected only by rags.

Washington pulled his horse to the side so he could watch the column maneuver into position. They had reached the rendezvous point, now all they could do was wait.

His aid rode up to his side, "General, we have not had any word, yet, from General Nathaniel Green. Our scouts are still out, but coming this far without word does not seem promising."

Washington leaned over and patted the neck of his Arabian, Blueskin. Colonel Tasker, from Maryland, had given him the magnificent horse as a gift when the continental congress had unanimously appointed him commander-in-chief of the colonial forces. He noticed that Blueskin's white hair coat blended in almost exactly with the snow at their feet.

"General Green may have had some difficulty getting his artillery across the river. We will give him some more time. At the very least I expect to hear news of his progress soon," said Washington.

"With all due respect, General, time is swiftly escaping us. It will be dawn before we know it. If the Hessians see us coming, we will lose every advantage we just worked for. They will be impossible to defeat in open battle." The aide sounded nervous.

"*Worry is the interest paid by those who borrow trouble*, son. We have not been borrowing trouble; we have been outmaneuvering it. We have time yet. Do not despair." Washington gave him a sly glance, "Now cheer up, *I would rather be alone than in bad company.*"

Blushing, the aid offered, "Of course, sir. My apologies, I must have let the cold get to me. I was not thinking straight."

Washington chuckled, "*It is better to offer no excuse than a bad one.* Now get on down to the crossroads and see if we have any of Greene's troops headed our way."

His aide delivered a crisp salute and took off in a gallop.

WASHINGTON WASN'T TRYING to be hard on the boy. He reminded him of himself back when he first joined the military, back in the Virginia Regiment. During the French and Indian War, his superior officers had been hard on him. Now he appreciated those lessons, and recognized them for what they were—mentorship.

He could hear his men fidgeting, restless in the piercing cold. He even thought he could hear teeth chattering. For an instant, he remembered the warmth of Barbados. It was the only time he had traveled outside the colonies. He remembered the warm sun and the sandy beaches, essentially the opposite of his current conditions.

His hand came to his cheek; he found the pock-mark scars left there from smallpox he had contracted on that island in the West Indies. That paradise had come with high cost. Still, at least it was warm.

The sound of horse hooves and creaking wagon wheels started to creep out of the darkness to his South. Within seconds, patriots on horseback started to materialize. It was Greene, Washington's most gifted and dependable officer. He brought with him the cannon he had captured with the help of Ethan Allen and his Green Mountain Boys at Ft. Ticonderoga.

"Glad to have you join us, General Greene." Washington extended his hand. "I was worried that I might need to write a formal invitation to have you join us for this little venture."

"Well, sir, you did. I wouldn't call it an invitation so much as a direct order." Green squeezed the outstretched hand.

"Apologies for our delay. The river was fighting us something fierce. Nearly lost a cannon, but we were able to prevent disaster. We did lose two men to exposure. Two good men, sir, all due to the cold." He said the last part with regret.

"That saddens me, general. I grieve for their loss. Make no mistake though, we will ensure it was not a sacrifice made in vain. You are familiar with the name of this operation. Aren't you? I felt it only appropriate." Washington's chest filled with determination.

"*Victory or Death*. That was the name, wasn't it, sir?" answered Greene.

"Indeed, victory or death, that exactly summarizes the stakes of this operation. America is in desperate need of a victory. The entire Revolution hangs by a thread. Congress and the people are weary and thus far our colonial army has been abused and defeated by British forces. Spirits are low across the 13 colonies. Trenton will be a turning point in this war. It must be a turning point if we hope to have further re-enlistments and support for our revolutionaries."

"Now, let us get the column moving, ride with me, general, as we approach the Hessian position." Washington spurred his horse.

Orders went out and soldiers started to get up, standing on numb feet. They hefted their packs and rifles and started down the road, headed toward what they knew could be a vicious battle. Most of them just hoped the storm would relent, otherwise, they might all be frozen before the first cannon fired.

"DID YOU KNOW I COME from a family of six children?" Washington and Greene were riding side by side down the dark path.

"No, sir, I cannot say that I was aware of that. Why do you mention it?"

Washington's silhouette bobbed as Blueskin trotted forward, "My mother raised all six of us. *All I am I owe to my mother. I attribute my success in life to the moral, intellectual and physical education I received from her.*"

He continued, "she taught us to *be courteous to all, but intimate with few, and let those few be well tried before you give them your confidence. True friendship is a plant of slow growth, and must undergo and withstand the shocks of adversity before it is entitled to* **appellation**."

Washington looked over to Greene, "I would say we have endured the shocks of adversity together, wouldn't you?"

Greene had to agree. "Certainly, we have been traveling a long and difficult road, sir. It feels like a lifetime ago that we were protesting King George III's Townshend Acts and then after the Boston Tea Party, those bloody Coercive Acts."

"You put it best, General Washington, those acts were indeed an intolerable '*invasion of our Rights and Privileges.*' We have been together since before the continental congress appointed us. Many—present company included—appreciated how you refused a salary for your services as commander-in-chief."

Greene gave a smile, "I hope you don't think me greedy for accepting a salary."

Washington suppressed a laugh, "Of course not, of course not. I only wish we could pay you and all of these patriots more for what they are doing."

"Back to my point though, I asked to ride with you because I wanted to tell you something. First, that after all you have done and continue to do, I consider you a dear friend." He paused to reinforce his sincerity.

"Second, if this attack on the Hessians—some might call it a **gambit**—if it proves unsuccessful, *I beg it may be remembered by every gentleman that I declare with the utmost sincerity, I do not think myself equal to the command I am honored with.*"

Washington's brought a fist to his chest. "If we should fail, the blame is mine and mine alone."

General Greene looked to his commander and admired his blend of nobility and humility. Here was a man without avarice, a man who wished to lead soldiers and serve his country. This was a man he would follow into any battle, no matter the odds.

OPERATION VICTORY OR Death's surprise attack worked better than anticipated. The Hessians were caught off guard and by battle's end Washington had secured more than 850 prisoners and, crucially, all of their supplies.

General George Washington went on to help the nation win its war for independence and he became the first president of the United States. His contemporaries remembered him as *"First in war, first in peace, first in the hearts of his countrymen."*

He was the father of this nation and taught: *"In politics as in philosophy, my tenets are few and simple. The leading one of which, and indeed that which embraces most others, is to be honest and just ourselves and to exact it from others, meddling as little as possible in their affairs where our own are not involved. If this maxim was generally adopted, wars would cease and our swords would soon be converted into reap hooks and our harvests be more peaceful, abundant, and happy."*

"Human happiness and moral duty are inseparably connected."

"I hope I shall possess firmness and virtue enough to maintain what I consider the most enviable of all titles, the character of an honest man."

Nobility was Washington's defining attribute. His high moral qualities set him apart from all others and earned the respect of the Continental Congress. We would do well to follow his example and act nobly in our daily lives.

15. ORDERLINESS of NASA

Diligent cleanliness, being well arranged
and organized.

O

"There is an orderliness in the universe. There is an unalterable law governing everything and every being that exists or lives. It is no blind law; for no blind law can govern the conduct of living beings." – Gandhi

Tranquility Base, The Moon, 1969

The spacesuit made it difficult to move; it wasn't designed with **dexterity** as its primary purpose. Still, Neal Armstrong was able to raise his arm, and then his thumb, before his helmet's visor. He used his extended thumb to cover the little blue dot hovering above the lunar surface—238,900 miles away.

Even though he never felt so isolated, so distant from humanity, Earth was listening. Just a few moments before, as he stepped off the lunar module's steps onto the moon's powdery surface, he uttered the line that he had carefully chosen.

"That's one small step for a man, one giant leap for mankind."

He knew millions were listening to his voice. He knew this was a seminal moment in human history. But in that instant, standing there covering the earth with his thumb, he felt small and alone, positively microscopic compared to the infinite expanse that surrounded and overwhelmed him.

It would be another 18 minutes until Buzz would be joining him on the surface. The next little while would be filled with unfathomable solitude. He surveyed the landscape in both directions, having to turn his whole body to do so.

"Magnificent desolation."

Buzz was right; it was magnificent. Wide flat plateaus suddenly met towering mountains caused by meteoric craters. Rocks, some the size of boulders and others the size of pebbles, were scattered in every direction, most of them in the exact same location where they landed thousands of years ago.

He began moving around the lunar module, getting a better take on where they landed. The gravity here was $1/6^{th}$ that of Earth, so he bounded from step to step, suddenly feeling like he could leap over a skyscraper if he wished.

On the far side of the lander, he saw a rock that was oddly smooth, not jagged and broken like those around it. The rock reminded him of the stones he used to skip with his youngest son Mark, back at the lake near Ellington Air Force Base in Texas.

The thought of Mark made him smile. He was just a boy. He remembered their last conversation.

"DAD, WHAT WOULD HAPPEN if you fell out of the lander without your spacesuit? The kids at school say that you would explode, that your blood would instantly boil." Mark looked horrified.

Neil tried not to laugh, "Hold on, hold on, son. No one is going to be falling out of any spaceships on this mission. I made it back from the Gemini mission just fine, didn't I?"

Mark pressed him. "Well, what if it did happen? What if you get hit by a space rock and rip your spacesuit? What if you fall and break that face shield thing? Then what, would you explode?"

"Absolutely not, I would not explode, son. My blood would not boil. Your friends are just teasing you. Plus, our suits are specifically designed to protect us from everything you described." Neil answered.

"Still, what would happen if it did." Mark looked down.

"Well, if it did—which it never would—but if it did, I suppose whatever part of me was exposed would immediately be flash frozen. Space is very cold. Then, there would be ebullism. That's when the nitrogen in the blood near the surface of the skin collects itself into little bubbles and expands, puffing up to twice their normal size. I would end up with a Mickey Mouse hand if I took my glove off." He held his hand up and splayed his fingers as he spoke.

"But what if it was your helmet; what if your face shield broke?"

"That would be tricky. I would need to immediately breathe all of the air out of my body, otherwise, the vacuum of space would rupture my lungs. It's the same thing that would happen to a scuba diver if they ascended too quickly."

His son asked sincerely, "How long would you have? How long could you survive?"

"I guess I would have around 15 seconds before I lost consciousness. Even then, I would be okay if my buddies got me back in the ship within two minutes. I'd probably have a bit of sunburn on my face though, because of the sun's radiation. Now, any more crazy questions before I put you to bed?"

"Just one, Dad, do you think heaven is up there where you're going? Do you think that you'll be closer to Karen?" Mark's head was leaning on his father's chest as he spoke.

His son's tender voice continued. "Is she up there? Why did she even have to go?"

Neil felt a wave of sadness course through him. He could not hear her name without feeling like his whole world was collapsing. She was perfect, an angel, they hadn't deserved her. Karen was always smiling, always laughing. When they found out she had a tumor no one could believe it. She seemed so filled with vitality.

But the tumor was real and within months his precious, perfect baby girl was gone. Even years later the pain was too much to bear, he had to keep it buried. Neil didn't want Mark to know just how raw, **visceral**, and profound Karen's loss was on him.

"Definitely. She is definitely up there, son. Everything happens for a reason. There is an order to the universe, even if we can't fully understand it. Tell you what, when I get there, I'll say a prayer and make sure she knows you're thinking of her; how about that?" Neil held back his tears as he tucked Mark into bed.

STATIC CRACKLED INTO his headset. "Hey there spaceman, did you miss me?" Buzz was descending the lunar module's ladder as he spoke.

Neil gave Buzz a salute as he joined him in the moon dust. "Just doing a bit of exploring. That's all."

"But of course, my friend. You know, Neil, *the urge to explore has propelled evolution since the first water creatures reconnoitered the land. Like all living systems, cultures cannot remain static; they evolve or decline. They explore or expire.* That drive brought us here."

Buzz looked out into the vast starlit expanse of space, "who knows how much further it will take us."

"Waxing eloquent in your old age there, Buzz. If only Collins could partake in that wisdom but alas, he is up there in orbit, manning the Columbia command module. He's really missing out." Neil joked with his shipmate.

They were both looking out at the earth now. "Guilty as charged. But can you blame me? Look at that." The Earth was bright and clear, four times the size of a full moon as seen from Earth. "That's our home back there, *a brilliant jewel in the black velvet sky.*"

The white spacesuits of the two astronauts contrasted vividly with the deep, dark gray surrounding them.

"I have to admit, Neil, being out here, I feel just as scared as I am excited. How do you feel? I mean, you nearly lost the entire wing off of your jet when you were flying an armed reconnaissance mission back in the Korean War. How do your feelings, standing here, compare to that?" Buzz asked.

"I'm almost too overwhelmed by the mystery and wonder of it all to feel scared. *There is still so much more that we don't understand. Mystery creates wonder, and wonder is the basis of man's desire to understand.*" Neil replied.

Buzz took a few additional steps forward. "I guess I feel the same way. It is overwhelming, but it is also beautiful. All of those stars, all of those planets in their perfect orbits, all of those galaxies, there is an underlying orderliness to it all. The real beauty of life is found in its orderliness."

The two spacemen spent the next two hours together outside the spacecraft and collected 47.5 pounds of lunar material to bring back to Earth. As they made their way back to the lunar module, Neil paused and allowed Buzz to get ahead of him.

"Everything good, buddy?" Buzz asked.

"Yeah, yeah I'm good. I just need one more minute. There is something that I still need to do. Something I promised my son I would do." Neil could sense Buzz shrug inside his suit and then continue on.

NEIL ARMSTRONG BEGAN a slow circular scan, turning his whole body as he went. With the Earth, Buzz, and the lunar module all at his back, he looked up. Stars, trillions upon trillions of stars, overflowed his field of view as far as his mortal eyes could see. Some were just pinpricks of light, millions of light-years away. Others were blazing so bright he had to resist the urge to shade his eyes. Their radiance covered the entire spectrum of light.

"Your brother wanted me to tell you he misses you, that he loves you, Karen." Emotion started to make his cheeks feel warm.

"But you know that already, don't you? I miss you too, we all do. We love you. We always will."

Then, in brilliant **resplendence**, one of the stars seemed to twinkle brighter than the rest.

THE APOLLO 11 SPACEFLIGHT was a tremendous success. Men had landed on the Moon. After eight days in space, the astronauts returned to Earth and splashed down in the Pacific Ocean. Left back on the moon was a simple plaque. It read, "Here men from the planet Earth first set foot upon the Moon. July 1969 AD. We came in peace for all mankind."

Neil Armstrong and Buzz Aldrin became famous for their daring feat. Buzz shared counsel with the youth of the day saying, *"Some people don't like to admit that they have failed or that they have not yet achieved their goals or lived up to their own expectations. But failure is not a sign of weakness. It is a sign that you are alive and growing."*

"Fear paralyzes in many ways, but especially if it keeps you from responding wisely and intelligently to challenges. The only way to overcome your fears is to face them head-on."

"Choose your heroes wisely, and be careful who you idolize. Why? Simple: you will become like the people with whom you most often associate."

Orderliness was essential for the crew of the Apollo 11. Their spacecraft required **vigilant** cleanliness. They had to keep track of their fuel, oxygen, and supplies meticulously. On a grander scale, they were exposed to the wonder of the cosmos and received a first-hand glimpse at the orderliness of the universe.

16. PERSEVERANCE of Ed Coan

Persistence despite difficulty or delay in achieving success.

"The key to powerlifting success is regular, long term, re-peated behavior."- Ed Coan

IPF World Championship Pori, Finland 1995

N o one thought he could do it. The stainless-steel, seven-foot barbell loomed above the entire audience at the International Powerlifting Federation's World Championships. Its sleeves had no room to spare. Plate after plate after plate was loaded until barely enough space remained for the safety collars.

The barbell weighed a gargantuan 1,000 pounds.

Ed Coan approached the platform and some in the audience gasped. The World Championship's competitors were of all shapes and sizes, but most were massive, lumbering hulks. A six-foot-tall man weighing 350 pounds would need to look up at most of his competition. A few of the lifters needed to crouch to enter doorways, their muscled shoulders and traps flexing as they hunched through the **threshold**.

The powerlifter who took the stage this time, however, was not a jacked, diesel semi-truck like the rest of those in the elite powerlifting ranks. Make no mistake, he was strong. His whole body was covered in an armor of thick corded muscle. Every step toward his mark caused ripples through his thighs, the quadriceps nearly hung over his knee caps. Still, none would accuse this man of being a giant.

Ed was 5'6".

His reputation preceded him to the barbell. Lifters the world over had heard of a new competitor who was winning competitions, earning the heaviest totals in all three of the lifts—the squat, bench press, and deadlift. He was beating competitors twice his size. Most competitions were won with a cool 50-pound margin, but Ed was often winning by 150, even up to 500 pounds. He was an unprecedented sensation in the powerlifting community.

Not everyone knew him though, someone from the front row snickered, "Look at that midget."

Ed barely heard the comment, his entire attention was centered like a laser beam on the barbell. Besides, he was used to derogatory comments flung his direction. Some people were sore losers and wanted to get in their jabs where they could. He was short, that was just a fact. Why should he feel embarrassed by something entirely beyond his control? When cruel words and bullying surrounded him, he said there was only one thing he needed to do.

"I prefer to let my lifting do the talking."

HIS FACE WAS STERN, emotionless, a face that Marcus Aurelias and the rest of the stoics would admire. The eyes though, there was fire burning in those eyes. **Ardor** emanated from a soul girded with determination and unstoppable will.

Most lifters had elaborate rituals to psyche themselves up for a lift, listening to raging rock music and jumping around. They got their adrenaline pumping by shouting, slapping each other in the face, or sniffing the eye-popping stench of ammonia smelling salts. They were barbarians preparing to go to battle on the platform.

Ed abstained from all such fanfare. He sat quietly waiting for his call, staring into the distance as he performed the lift in his mind over and over again. By the time he addressed the bar, he had already completed the lift with surgical precision countless times; all that was left was to take that vision and make it a reality.

"Everything is created twice." One of his high school wrestling coaches was a bit of a philosopher. "First you create it in your mind, then you create it in reality. You win in your mind, then you win on the mat."

His right hand, calloused and tough, reached up and grabbed the barbell. The index finger aligned itself precisely with the knurling. His left hand followed and mirrored his right. He started to squeeze the bar, feeling tension course through his fingers, hands, then forearms.

"Take your time. Focus on technique." His mind reminded him.

The setup was crucial to a successful lift. Ed had honed the routine through countless repetitions in training. Even with warm-up sets, he was precise in his setup. He often said, *"When you start to treat the light weights like heavy weights, the heavy weights will go up a lot easier."*

He glanced left and right, measuring his position to ensure he was dead center. Even though 1,000 pounds looked imposing, there was no doubt that he would make the lift. This was the culmination of months of deliberate linear progression. Every set rep weight exercise was planned out beforehand to get him where he wanted to go. He never deviated from it. Ed always planned his training with the end in mind.

Ed kept things simple. He was careful to not over-train. He knew that practice did not make perfect. Repeated bad form in practice would ingrain dangerous movement patterns. No, PERFECT practice makes perfect. Consistency and persistence were the hallmarks he lived by.

An outside observer would probably have considered his life boring. He once said, "*Without productive and repetitive grooves, patterns and work habits, I have no regularity and therefore cannot possibly optimize my physical progress. To improve, I need to do positive things on a regular and recurring basis.*"

"*Within this framework of constant regularity, I will change and tinker with the individual components: training, diet, rest, supplementation, nutrition, and the like. But my overall pattern of repeated positive behavior is constant and unchanging. The regularity provided by my home environment is the foundation onto which everything else is built.*"

HE WAS UNDER THE BAR now. The barbell resting firmly on the shelf created by his trapezius muscles, huge slabs of meat. Ed drew in a final breath, feeling his entire diaphragm surge with air, pressing into his lifting belt and forming a hyper-dense cushion of air around his spine.

The barbell lifted from the rack. Despite its 190,000 PSI tensile strength steel, the barbell bent slightly, 1,000 pounds was taking it to the limits of its capability. Ed took one meticulous step back, then another.

He was in position.

"Well, if your mind controls what your body does, I'm gonna keep my mind really happy." If Ed was calculating and determined in the gym, he was even more so during recovery. He rarely partied, never stayed up late watching movies or playing video games. He knew his body needed to rest so it could grow, so he slept. He slept more than any of his siblings or friends. He only ate food that would build muscle and he avoided beverages that could set him back, such as beer. Even as a teenager his mother had been impressed by his discipline.

"Why do you do it, Ed?" It was an honest question from a caring parent.

He remembered admiring Schwarzenegger and other bodybuilders who were popular in his youth. Something inside him craved the hard work that forged a herculean physique. He sensed the truth in Rippetoe's words that *"humans are not physically normal in the absence of hard physical effort...Strong people are harder to kill than weak people, and more useful in general."*

Ed descended with the barbell, every muscle in his body straining to keep him from being crushed by the relentless weight. He came all the way down into the bottom position, the tops of his thighs well below his knees. The three judges gave the signal that he had hit proper depth.

FEELING THE STRETCH in his hamstrings, Ed suddenly started to drive upwards with all of his might. Veins in his neck and forehead appeared like they might burst at any moment.

His mind was completely free of doubt, it focused solely on pressing the weight back up. For a millisecond, the words of Rollins flashed through his mind.

"The Iron never lies to you. You can walk outside and listen to all kinds of talk, get told that you're a god or a total turd. The Iron will always kick you the real deal. The Iron is the great reference point, the all-knowing perspective giver. Always there like a beacon in the pitch black. I have found the Iron to be my greatest friend. It never freaks out on me, never runs. Friends may come and go. But two hundred pounds is always two hundred pounds."

Here, at the world championships, 1,000 pounds was definitely 1,000 pounds.

With bated breath, the entire audience watched as the barbell inched upwards, smoothly, a glacier sliding through space. Then it was there, at the top, mounted on the shoulders of a man trembling in absolute and utter exertion.

Then it was over. Ed Coan had successfully squatted 1,000 pounds, over four and a half times his bodyweight.

ED WENT ON TO ACHIEVE career-best lifts of 585 in the bench press and 901 pounds in the deadlift. He won the world championships. Not only that, he went on to set 71 world records in powerlifting and remained at the top for over twenty years. What Lebron James is to basketball and Tiger Woods is to golf, Ed Coan is to powerlifting—except on an even higher scale.

That said, Ed's satisfaction is found in the process, not in defeating his opponents. The competition is between who he is today and who he was yesterday, not in relation to others. No trophies adorn his wall; he keeps most of them at his sisters' houses. It was never about the trophies or the records. It was about becoming the best, strongest version of himself.

Perseverance set Ed apart from the competition. He was not the biggest, the most experienced, or the most gifted lifter, yet he rose to the very top of elite powerlifting and remained there for decades because of his discipline and willingness to persevere.

17. QUIETNESS of Christ

Absence of noise or bustle; state of calm, tranquility, and peace.

*"Peace I give unto you...let not your heart be troubled, neither let it be afraid." -*Jesus Christ

Near the temple, Jerusalem, 30 AD

S imon Peter did not like the looks of things. The crowd that was gathering in the street was now headed their direction. The shouts and slurs coming from their ranks did not **portend** a friendly encounter.

"Master, perhaps it would be best if we departed, with haste." Peter tried to speak reverently, but the urgency of the situation crept into his tone.

Jesus was crouched low, speaking with a child that had come up to them. It struck Peter that children were always drawn to his teacher. It was as if their senses detected something important, something out of place and pure was nearby. He and the rest of the apostles had been gently **scolded** on more than one occasion for shooing the children away.

"Of such is the kingdom of God." He had told Peter. Christ's rebukes were always delivered with such love and compassion that he could not begrudge him. This time though, he was determined to get Jesus out of the street and away from the crowd. Christ never asked him to be his bodyguard, but Peter was glad to fill the role as best he could.

"Please, we really must go, the Pharisees are coming and they surely bring nothing but trouble with them. I would rather see you teaching something important than being abused by criticizers." Peter was practically begging now.

"Peace, be still, my friend. We will see what they have to say. Have faith." Christ patted the child on the head affectionately and then rose to his feet.

Those words, "Peace, be still" penetrated deep into Peter's heart. Those were the very words that Christ had used in one of the most miraculous experiences he had ever witnessed. They rang in his ears with divine power.

AFTER COUNTLESS HOURS ministering to the people, Peter had finally convinced Jesus to allow them to return to their ship and to embark on the next leg of their travels. Christ had fallen fast asleep as Peter and his brothers navigated the vessel. A storm, more ferocious than he had ever endured, suddenly rose up out of the sea and engulfed them in wind and rain.

The seasoned sailors worked frantically, securing sails and bailing water. The threat of sinking grew more and more real. Death by drowning seemed imminent.

Peter had gone to the hold of the ship to ensure Christ had not been injured during the violent rocking of the ship. To his surprise, his master was still fast asleep. He could not believe his eyes. The man must have been utterly exhausted.

Still, it struck him as a bit brash to attempt to sleep through a tempest. Besides, was he not worried about the welfare of his crew?

"*Master, carest thou not that we perish?*" Peter was shaking him awake now, they needed to get to the deck in case they had to abandon ship.

Instead of waking in a panic as any mortal would naturally react, Christ had calmly lifted himself from the sheets and moved up the steps. When he arrived on the deck he held a line to steady himself from the steep tilt of the ship and raised his other hand. Then he uttered the three words that Peter would never forget.

"*Peace, be still.*"

Christ had rebuked the storm. Suddenly, as though the storm clouds had been parted by an invisible mighty hand, light from the setting sun broke through. The seas calmed, too quickly to be natural. The waves didn't gradually decrease in size, bit by bit, until they eventually were mild. No, almost instantly, they ceased to rock the ship. Within moments the waters were still, calm, a sea of glass.

That was when Peter knew he was in the presence of something he could not fully grasp.

THE CROWD WAS UPON them, encircling Christ and his twelve disciples. Two Pharisees stepped forward, a woman wrestling against their hold. They cast the woman onto the ground at Jesus's feet.

"*This woman has been caught in the act of adultery. Now, in the law, Moses commanded us to stone such. What do you say about her?*" sneered the older of the two.

Jesus knelt beside the woman and helped her rise to a sitting position. Her arms were scratched and bruised from the scuffle. He took a moment and wrote something in the sand by her feet.

"Well, what do you say about her?" repeated the pharisee. Others in the crowd chimed in, "What say you? Come on, what say you?"

Christ looked up at them and rose to his feet, placing himself between the woman and her accusers. He noticed that the men had stones in their hands, they had come prepared to exact the law of Moses.

STONING WAS USED AS both punishment and deterrent for a variety of crimes in Israel. It had been this way for generations. The people enjoyed relative peace amongst themselves because of **ubiquitous** respect for the law. Stoning was the punishment for adultery, pure and simple.

Then the Romans came. They came with their legions and their chariots. They had conquered almost the entirety of the known world and with them came new laws and new judicial practices. Every Israelite was still trying to figure out how to navigate the balance of power between Hebrew tradition and Rome's unprecedented might.

Peter could sense the trap.

The Sadducees and Pharisees wanted Christ gone, he had threatened their power with the people and they could not abide his teachings. Word had already spread throughout the city that Christ taught simple principles, that he claimed his yoke was easy and his burden light. It was a major shift from the high demands of orthodox religious practice where even the number of steps you could take on the Sabbath were regulated.

"Thou shalt love the Lord thy God with all thy heart, and with all thy soul, and with all thy mind. This is the first and great commandment. And the second is like unto it, thou shalt love thy neighbor as thyself. On these two commandments hang all the law and the prophets."

Christ claimed to fulfill the law of Moses, he offered a higher law. The changes he sought were completely intolerable to Jewish leaders. Jesus did not even offer them relief from the oppression of Roman rule, he offered the complete opposite of military victory against their enemy.

"Ye have heard that it hath been said, thou shalt love thy neighbor, and hate thine enemy. But I say unto you, love your enemies, bless them that curse you, do good to them that hate you, and pray for them which despitefully use you, and persecute you."

Peter knew that if the Pharisees could get Christ to agree that stoning was the answer, they could turn him into the Romans for violating their laws and usurping their authority. Rome let their subjects have their religion—but never at the expense of Roman law.

If Christ told them to turn her over to Roman authorities, they would be able to use that as evidence that he had no respect for Hebrew tradition and authority. They could discredit him with the very people that were starting to flock toward his teachings.

Peter did not see a way out of this one, he wished that Jesus had just listened to him. They could have been long gone and avoided this entire **sordid** affair. But then he remembered those words, "Peace, be still."

He held his tongue and watched his master.

CHRIST PEERED SOLEMNLY into the eyes of each man before him, individually, the look a mixture of disappointment and compassion. Then he spoke, his voice rising clear and pure, cutting through the **cacophony** of the crowd like a razor.

"Let him who is without sin among you be the first to throw a stone at her."

Then, Christ stepped aside and revealed what he had written in the earth. He knelt again by the woman and resumed writing.

The eldest Pharisee, who offered the original accusation, was about to speak again. Then he noticed the words on the ground.

IT WAS HIS NAME. CHRIST did not know him, they had never even met, yet he had written his name in the sand. Then the Pharisee remembered the words of Jeremiah, that the names of those who turn away from God shall be written in the earth, for they have forsaken the Lord, the fountain of living water.

The list of names in the sand was growing, it was the names of every single accuser, written from eldest to youngest. Each man gasped and felt startled when they recognized their name, the words from Jeremiah ringing in their souls. They were filled with a recognition of their hypocrisy and evil intent.

One by one, beginning with the eldest Pharisee, they dropped their rocks and departed. In just a few minutes, what was once a wild and raucous street was now a place of quiet tranquility.

Christ looked to the woman and quietly asked, *"Where are they? Is there no one to condemn you?"*

Tears welled up in her eyes and she replied, *"No one, Lord."*

Jesus said, *"Neither do I condemn you; go, and sin no more."*

Peter watched as the woman meekly departed. Then he saw Christ rise to his feet and a hint of a smile crossed his lips. "Peter, did you not ask to see something important taught?"

He remembered his words before the crowd arrived and he nodded to his master.

Christ's smile was full now, pure and well-meaning. *"Ask, and it shall be given you; seek, and ye shall find; knock, and it shall be opened unto you."*

JESUS CHRIST WAS A radical in his day. Not in the context of destroying organized Hebrew traditions, but in the original meaning of the word radical. The Roman word *radicalis* meant "root" or "forming the root." Christ quietly brought attention back to the fundamental roots of religion—love. He taught love for God, oneself, and one's neighbor.

Abraham Joshua Heschel noted candidly, *"It is customary to blame secular science and anti-religious philosophy for the eclipse of religion in modern society. It would be more honest to blame religion for its own defeats. Religion declined not because it was refuted, but because it became irrelevant, dull, oppressive, **insipid.**"*

He continued, *"When faith is completely replaced by creed, worship by discipline, love by habit; when the crisis of today is ig-*

nored because of the splendor of the past; when faith becomes an heirloom rather than a living fountain; when religion speaks only in the name of authority rather than with the voice of compassion—its message becomes meaningless."

Quietness accompanied Christ during his earthly ministry. His countenance emanated purity and confidence. His teachings brought people closer to God and gave them a deeper sense of meaning and purpose. Jesus Christ became known as the Prince of Peace, an apt title indeed.

18. RESPONSIBILITY of Curie

Ability to act correctly and make decisions on your own; your duty.

"Nothing in life is to be feared, it is only to be under-stood. Now is the time to understand more, so that we may fear less." – Marie Curie

Paris, France 1906

"**P**ierre, it's my least favorite thing in the world," she had to admit it, going to parties was just about her least favorite way to spend her free time. Marie Curie had her arm interlaced with her husband as they walked up the steps of the Palais Garnier. The invitation to the soirée had come as a bit of a surprise. It took her husband two full weeks to convince her to accept the invitation.

The 1,979 seat opera house rose majestically before them. It was opened in 1875 for the Paris Opera and tonight it hosted a gathering of France's social elite. All of the wealthiest families would be present, along with leaders in government, business, even religion. Marie didn't know the exact purpose of the gathering; she knew there was always an excuse for someone to throw an **extravagant** party.

Arm in arm, they entered through the massive entrance and stepped onto the polished floor and her breath caught as the entire room came into view. It was awe-inspiring. Perfect marble pillars extended up into the distant ceiling of the massive foyer. Even with throngs of socialites milling about, the room felt colossal.

The grand staircase was clearly the centerpiece of the room, its marble steps rising out of the crowd and splitting into two separate staircases like a leviathan rising from the deep. Gold ornamentation and sculptures covered almost every surface. The **opulence** was too well crafted to offend the eye, she had to appreciate the product of what must have been hundreds of thousands of hours of labor.

Vibrant colored gowns blossomed like flowers in every direction. Ornate hats and bows adorned the crowns of nearly every woman. Marie felt positively bland in contrast to her surroundings. In her signature black dress, she was a duckling lost in a sea of peacocks.

"WHY MARIE, HOW ABSOLUTELY wonderful of you to join us." It was Lady Evelyn, the wife of the largest landowner in Versailles.

"Thank you, madam. My husband and I were flattered to receive an invitation."

Evelyn gave a look of shock, "How could we possibly overlook inviting our very own winner of the Nobel Prize? The very first woman to win the prize, I might add."

Marie blushed, genuinely embarrassed by the attention. She noticed that a few other ladies were approaching them. Evelyn drew a crowd like a magnet draws ferromagnetic particles. It did not seem like she ever minded the attention—even if half of those surrounding her were **sycophants** hoping to improve their station in life.

Pierre noticed a few gentlemen he'd met at the university. "Pardon me, dear, forgive me if I leave you to Evelyn for a while." Before she could reply, he was off, weaving through the crowd.

"Well, well, who do we have here?" Antoinette sidled up to Evelyn and looked Marie up and down disapprovingly.

"Managed to break free from the laboratory to mingle with the lay folk, have we?" Her comment had no kindness in it. "Did you come directly from the laboratory?"

Marie looked down at her dress and felt unsure of how to respond, she had not come to argue with the wealthy. "I suppose I could have found a more colorful dress." Then she exposed one of her feet, shod in simple slippers.

"On the other hand, I'm very happy with my choice of footwear. *You'll never make me believe women were made to walk on stilts.*" Marie hoped humor might diffuse the tension.

CELESTE JOINED THE conversation; she was Antoinette's younger sister and was somehow less amicable—if that was even possible. "Our very own Nobel Prize Winner. It must be nice getting all of that recognition for your hard work. What was it you did again? You discovered a new element, wasn't it?"

"Yes, polonium and radium, my research focuses on radioactivity and its medical applications."

"Hmm, I wonder what it must be like spending all of my time away from my children playing with laboratory equipment and then getting awards. Has it been easy **abdicating** your responsibilities as a mother?" Celeste was making an accusation more than asking a question.

"You are not the first to present that question, Celeste. *I have frequently been questioned, especially by women like you, of how I could reconcile family life with a scientific career. Well, it has not been easy.*" Marie was trying to maintain her composure.

Marie tried to change the subject, "*Perhaps we could be less curious about people and more curious about ideas.* I admit myself that I am still trying to find a healthy balance of work and family. *I try not to concern myself with perfection. I say, have no fear of perfection; we'll never reach it.*"

"Why not just make a choice, Marie? Just choose between your children or science. Why not leave the laboratory with the men where it belongs?" Antoinette wouldn't let the conversation go.

"I suppose it comes back to responsibility. There are very few researchers in my field and I have much that I can still contribute. *Life is not easy for me, or any of us. But what of that? We must have perseverance and above all confidence in ourselves. We must believe that we are gifted for something and that this thing must be attained.*" Marie hoped that was a satisfactory response.

Evelyn tried to interject; the awkwardness was starting to reach an intolerable level. Before she could get a word in, Celeste asked, "Surely the Science could continue pressing forward without the great Marie Curie. Do you truly think so highly of yourself to believe you are **indispensable**?"

Before responding, Marie paused a moment. Despite the barbed nature of the question, Marie felt its legitimacy. "Yes, science would carry on. *Sometimes my courage fails me, and I think I ought to stop working, live in the country and devote myself to gardening. But I am held by a thousand bonds, and I don't know when I shall be able to arrange things otherwise. Nor do I know whether, even by writing scientific books, I could live with-out the laboratory."*

With confidence, Marie looked at Celeste and Antoinette and said, "I should add; *one of the first principles I live by is to never let one's self be beaten down by persons or events.* So, if you will kindly excuse me." She started to turn away. She just wanted to find Pierre.

Evelyn finally had her chance. "Marie, wait, please. You must forgive these **impetuous** sisters; they mean no real harm. Sometimes they forget to censor the thoughts that churn in their silly heads."

Antoinette and Celeste tried to conceal their embarrassment at Evelyn calling them out, "She is right, we did not mean to offend."

"No real harm done. We all have room to improve. *You cannot hope to build a better world without improving the individual. To that end, each of us must work for his own improvement, and at the same time share a general responsibility for all humanity, our particular duty being to aid those to whom we think we can be most useful."* Marie offered.

"I just love that idea, it is wisdom to be sure." Evelyn grabbed Marie about the shoulders. "Now, shall we go and see where our husbands have absconded themselves?"

"Yes, gladly, I would be delighted by that." Marie was glad to part ways from the sisters. Truly, walking among the throngs of high society left her feeling more like an immigrant than she had ever felt when she first moved to Paris from Poland. Surrounded by such luxury and excess, she was not with her people.

She knew that when one studied strongly radioactive substances special precautions must be taken. Dust, the air of the room, and one's clothes, all become radioactive. Dealing with these influential members of high society, in a small way, reminded her of dealing with radioactive materials. Their influence could rub off on you. With safe doses it could be used for good, to do X-rays and provide medical treatment.

An unhealthy dose would kill you, slowly, subtly, and surely.

MARIE CURIE WENT ON to earn yet another Nobel Prize. She was the first person and only woman to win the prestigious award twice. Not only that, but she earned the award in two different fields. Her pioneering research on radioactivity led to advancements in the medical field that have saved countless lives. Her work led to the establishment of the field of radiation therapy for cancer.

Sadly, her exposure to radiation caused her to contract leukemia and she died at the relatively young age of 66. In recognition of her tremendous accomplishments, she became the first woman to be entombed on her own merits in Paris' Pantheon.

Marie offered sage counsel: *"I was taught that the way of progress is neither swift nor easy."*

"You must never be fearful of what you are doing when it is right"

Responsibility drove Marie Curie forward in her research. She felt it was her duty to advance the science of her field. Her courage and perseverance created a legacy that lasts to this day. She took her responsibility seriously.

19. SPARTAN Leonidas

Indifference to comfort or luxury, strict self-discipline; laconic.

S

"Be brave my heart. Plant your feet and square your shoulders to the enemy. Meet him among the man-killing spears. Hold your ground. In victory, do not brag. In defeat, do not weep." -Archilochus

Thermopylae, Greece 480 BC

LEONIDAS HAD FALLEN. The great warrior-king was lying in the sand and wounded, a mere hundred meters beyond the Spartan line that held the narrow pass of Thermopylae. He and a small band had been returning from a raid on the camp of Xerxes. Their mission was to slay the self-proclaimed king of kings in his own tent.

Stealth carried Leonidas and his chosen men silently to the center of the Persian position. Their covert skills were honed since childhood, every Spartan had to complete the upbringing—the Agoge. Regardless of bloodline, each boy had to survive the right of passage's **austerity**.

During the Agoge there were no beds, no talking, each boy allowed a single tunic. One test required they run ten miles with a mouthful of water, at the completion of the race all had to spit the water out. Whoever had succumbed to temptation and quenched their thirst was scourged by a whip.

Rather than break their silence, some boys would die before they would cry out during the whipping.

The Spartans infiltrated to the Persian king's very bedchamber, but Xerxes was a paranoid man. His best soldiers, the immortals, guarded their emperor and the assassination was thwarted.

Xerxes pursued Leonidas with cavalry and his immortals, but the Spartans possessed a fleetness of foot that belied their thick muscular physiques. They had made it almost entirely back to the Spartan line before the cavalry caught up to them and cut down their king.

It was the seventh day.

FOR SEVEN DAYS A SMALL band of Greeks, led by Leonidas and 300 of his best warriors, held the pass at Thermopylae—The Hot Gates. Persia wished yet again to expand its empire and had amassed an army of over 300,000 troops. Before resorting to violence, Xerxes sent emissaries bearing gifts and an offer of peaceful abdication of rule into his hands.

The emissaries brought promises of wealth, riches, untold pleasures if they would but pay tribute to their god-king. Representatives of Athens, Thrace, and all of the city-states were gathered to hear the message. Leonidas, "son of the lion" had attended himself, accompanied by his childhood friend Dienekes. They listened to the entreaty skeptically.

Dienekes looked to his king and wondered how he would respond to the Persian's request. He remembered the tales of his grandfather. How, years before, Philip of Macedon and his son Alexander the Great, had threatened to invade and conquer Sparta if she did not surrender.

Their message said, "*If I invade Laconia you will be destroyed, never to rise again.*" The Spartans replied with one word.

"*If.*"

Frustrated, King Philip asked, "*Should the Macedonian army come to Sparta as a friend or a foe?*" laying down the ultimatum of submission or conquest. Leonidas's forefather gave a simple reply.

"*Neither.*"

Dienekes could tell Leonidas was not overly impressed by the Persian's deal. He was a Spartan and represented the most feared army in all of Greece. Spartans were self-sufficient and willingly chose a life of minimalism. They despised luxury and lived in a city that contained neither walls nor extravagant buildings. Spartan peers had no occupation but warrior, their society was bound together by honor and tradition.

It was a striking contrast. The Persians with their wine and silk versus the Spartans with their wool and pig's blood stew. Once, an ambassador who ate at a public mess, remarked, "*Now I know why the Spartans do not fear death.*" It was wealth and possession versus honor and shared sacrifice.

Leonidas addressed the group, "*How far the Persians have come to rob us of our poverty.*"

The Persian eyed him, annoyed by the **petulance**. "Careful what you say, Spartan. This offer will come only once. I warn you, Xerxes—our god-king—has innumerable hosts of soldiers who will gladly fight and die for him."

"And *I would die for any one of mine.*" Leonidas crossed his arms and leaned back against a sandstone pillar.

"So, war is it? For the sake of your foolish pride, you will sacrifice your entire nation? Xerxes will **raze** every last one of your cities to the ground. His armies will march on Greece by the thousands and hundreds of thousands." The Persian was shaking his fists, his brow strained in fury.

In a flash, Leonidas sprang from his seemingly relaxed position against the pillar. He drew his *xiphos* short sword and held the tip against the Persian's neck, a trickle of blood started to seep onto the blade.

"We Spartans do not ask how many are the enemy," he inspected the Persian coolly, *"but where they are."*

Dienekes had his sword drawn as well, he was partly relieved when his king released the envoy. The Persian held his throat and rasped angrily, "You're dead, you're all dead. Just wait, Xerxes will come and smash your puny armies, *his arrows will blot out the sun."*

As they walked away Dienekes could not resist. He turned back to the Persian and bowed with a smile, *"Then we shall fight in the shade."*

Xerxes had come, his Armies did seem innumerable. The clouds of dust churned up by his cavalry and his war elephants extended far into the sky and filled the horizon as far as the eye could see. The scouts identified over 300,000 troops hailing from all parts of the empire, and that was just counting what they could see.

When the Persians realized that a small band of Greeks blocked the narrow pass that led into the mainland, Xerxes offered one last gracious opportunity. Every Spartan and Greek present would walk away with their lives, free to return to their homelands, if they but lay down their weapons.

Leonidas, true to his laconic roots countered. *"Molan Labe,* come and take them."

NOW HIS KING LAY BEFORE him, separated by a growing wall of Persians. Treachery had given the Persians the advantage. Ephialtes—a Greek traitor—brought a Persian general to a mountain track that led to the rear of the Greeks.

In response, Leonidas ordered the Greek forces to withdraw and live to fight another day. Only his 300 and a few others would remain to hold the pass until they were safely away.

Dienekes had led three charges to try and recover his king, his friend. Each time they had almost reached Leonidas but were overwhelmed by the countless number of Persians. He had managed to gather what remained of the Spartan forces.

They were now organized in a tight formation, their large *hoplon* shields interlocked. His calloused hands gripped the handle, located near the shield's edge. A leather strap wrapped over his forearm, locking the shield in place.

It was his father's shield and his father's shield before that. He would not dishonor this warrior's heirloom. Before departing for battle, Queen Gorgon had offered the infamous line, *"Come back with your shield or on it."*

The strength of the phalanx was in their unity, the shield there to protect the brother at their side. It allowed a small force to take on much greater numbers effectively. Dienekes shouted to his formation as they advanced, *"Fight for this alone, the man who stands at your shoulder. He is everything and everything is contained within him."* Then he peered out from behind the bronze cheek plates of his helmet and prayed.

"Lord, let me not prove unworthy of my brothers."

Persians crushed into the wall of forged bronze shields. The wall held, and then—as one—the Spartans pushed forward and knocked the line of Persians back on their heels. Spears suddenly thrust from behind the shields and impaled the unsuspecting attackers. The light armor and wicker shields of the Persians were no match for the razor-sharp points of the phalanx's *doru* spears.

Sensing this could be their last chance to recover their king, the Spartans pressed forward, an unstoppable force cutting through a sea of spikes and swords. More than 10,000 Persian infantry lay dead, bodies stacked on top of bodies. Dienekes had to be careful not to stumble as they stepped on top of slippery flesh. He wondered if they would ever make it through, they had been fighting non-stop for days and their bodies were drawing energy from empty stores.

The Phalanx finally reached Leonidas. Their king was on the ground, his red cape spread out around him. He had fallen protecting one of his warriors whose arm had been lost in the night raid. Dienekes called to the phalanx and it changed its shape, forming the turtle formation around their fallen king.

Spartan shields closed around Leonidas and Dienekes knelt beside him. The exhausted warriors could hear the Persians regrouping and surrounding their informidable position.

LEONIDAS BARELY CLUNG to life. Dienekes removed his friend's helmet, noticing that the horsehair crest had been nearly cut from its crown. The king winced in pain, broken ribs and multiple stab wounds made every breath a struggle.

"I've always liked your name, Dienekes," said the king. "*Unbroken*. It suits you, just like it suits our entire people."

"Yes, my king. Rest easy now, you are among friends, your brothers. We would not leave you out there on the field to have all the fun by yourself. We are together now and shall remain so until this is over." Dienekes could not keep the tears from welling up in his eyes.

Leonidas, despite the pain, looked into the eyes of his friend, the man with whom he had survived the Agoge so many years ago.

"Fear not brother. This battle has fulfilled its purpose and Greece will have a fighting chance tomorrow." The Persian advance could be heard, hordes of screaming soldiers charging their meager formation.

Leonidas grimaced and leaned up onto his elbow. He reached up and placed his hand on the neck of Dienekes, pulling him down so their foreheads met. Eyes closed, he said, "Thank you for coming for me, my brother. Greece will survive tomorrow, but we have no need to concern ourselves with that, *for tonight we dine in hades.*"

THE PERSIANS EVENTUALLY broke the Phalanx and slaughtered the Spartans to the last man. The Spartans at Thermopylae may have lost their lives, but they succeeded in their mission and Greece had the chance to gather its armies and repel the invading Persian force.

Spartans took pride in their warrior culture and held contempt for luxury. They refused to mince words and spoke their minds in a concise, honest manner. They were the original minimalists and chose the principles that they held in high esteem carefully. To live a spartan life is to live a life of purpose with limited distraction.

Be true to your ideals; be honest in your dealings with your fellow men; be fit and formidable—be a SPARTAN.

20. THANKFULLNESS of Keller

Feeling of being happy or grateful; showing appreciation.

"When one door of happiness closes, another opens; but often we look so long at the closed door that we do not see the one which has been opened for us." – Helen Keller

Tuscumbia, Alabama 1887

No one had more reason to be miserable than Helen Keller. Blind and deaf, she was at sea in a dense fog, unable to discern anything around her. Scarlet fever tried to kill her as a baby. Instead, it left her condemned to a life of uncertainty, fear, and misery.

Most children filled their days playing outside with their friends, swinging from trees and exploring the beauties of nature. Helen couldn't join them. She would never be able to play hide and seek, never be able to see the fiery sky at sunset or hear the soft **warble** of a songbird.

Her parents were proud people from strong Southern stock. It broke their hearts to see their daughter pass the days away slumped in a chair just staring into nothingness. Their attempts to engage with her were always met with frustration. Their neighbors told them it was a lost cause.

"A lost cause," that phrase carried some weight with her father, Arthur. He'd been a captain in the Confederate Army during the civil war. He knew something about lost causes. When he'd signed up to fight the Union troops, some neighbors warned him that the North was unbeatable. The Union had superior numbers, abundant resources, even extensive rail networks. There was no way that the South could stand a chance against the Northern **juggernaut**.

When cannons fired at Fort Sumter in Charleston Bay both Union and Confederacy unleashed the dogs of war. Alabama called upon Arthur's service. His wife, Catherine, could sense bloodshed on the horizon and asked him not go. He remembered the conversation.

"Kate, you know I must do this. I will not allow my neighbors and family to go into battle without me. The North says we are fighting to hang onto slavery. The South says we go to war to prove the sovereignty of individual states. But I go because I feel it is my duty."

"No Arthur, it is not your duty. You never signed a contract obligating yourself to military service. You don't owe anybody anything. You can't leave your family; you might be wounded or maimed. Worse yet, you might die. Please, you can't go," she begged.

"Darling, your own father, your flesh and blood, leads a Dixie Regiment. He is a general, Kate. Do you think I would ever be able to look him in the eye again if I sat this out? What would I say to him when he comes to visit, knowing I was nothing more than a yellow-bellied-coward?"

He could see Kate resigning herself to the situation. "You have my love and my blessing, but you will regret this decision."

Now, back from the war, he could see the wisdom in his wife's words. He did regret so much of what happened. 620,000 dead, countless more wounded and marked for life. He remembered the screams from the surgical tents, he remembered the bodies strewn about the field. Such waste, such terrible loss, almost an entire generation of Americans swept from the earth.

He did not regret it all. He was thankful for the lessons he had learned. His company of Alabama volunteers had been assigned to General Stonewall Jackson's Army. Through deft maneuver and discipline, Jackson's army defeated three separate Union Armies. The Shenandoah campaign was a marvel of modern warfare and he had been a part of it. They defied the odds and had won over and over again.

HE WAS THANKFUL FOR that lesson, that you can win despite terrible odds. He did not give up back when he was wearing that gray uniform, and he would not give up now. His daughter needed him, and he and Kate would not see her spend her life in misery.

They needed to get through to her, but they knew no amount of cuddling or kissing of her forehead was going to change anything. He and Kate had exhausted every resource trying to find a medical specialist who could assist them in this effort.

With the arrival of Anne Sullivan, they hoped their prayers were answered.

Anne was an astute individual, young and fresh-faced. She herself was visually impaired, but her bright mind was filled with a devotion to serving others, and she had ideas on how she could reach Helen. The first day was challenging, Helen could sense a stranger in her midst and had recoiled at Anne's touch. It took hours before she would let Anne even hold her hand.

Anne was deliberate though. She knew the process would not be easy. The goal was to help Helen communicate by spelling words into her hand with sign language. She saw that Helen was holding a doll, so she signed the letters "d-o-l-l" into her hand. Helen stared blankly back at her, not comprehending the message. Anne removed the doll and then placed it back in her hand and then spelled the letters again. They repeated the process until supper time.

Patience was critical, Anne knew that Helen did not know she was spelling words, or that words even existed. Still, she was satisfied when Helen started to mimic the letters, even if it was little more than a monkey-like imitation. It was progress, a small victory, and incremental progress was all that she could ask for.

After days of effort, Anne had the idea to take Helen to the garden and allow her to feel the sun's rays, to smell the fresh air, and to feel the cool caress of water upon her fingertips. She signed the letters for w-a-t-e-r into Helen's palm. She drew her hands through the water again and repeated the sign.

Suddenly, a misty consciousness of something forgotten broke through to Helen. She felt the thrill of realization, and somehow the mystery of language was revealed to her. She knew that w-a-t-e-r meant the wonderful cool something that was flowing over her hand. The living word awakened her soul, gave it light, hope, set it free.

HELEN'S NEWFOUND UNDERSTANDING gave her a voracious appetite for more. She begged Anne to bring her new objects, take her new places, give her new words to learn. The whole world was suddenly before her and she wished to no more be a stranger.

Arthur and Kate were spellbound by the sudden transformation. Their daughter, the lost cause, had emerged from a cocoon of solitude and was now a brilliant butterfly of vitality and learning. She was an inspiration; the whole process was a miracle of miracles.

Her parents were awed by Helen's ability to connect with the outside world. She would enjoy music not by listening to it with her eardrums like the rest of humanity, instead, she would feel the beat course through her. Though she could not see or hear animals, she found peace in petting their soft fur and feeling their breath on her cheek.

When Helen approached her father and asked if she could seek a degree at the university, he was reluctant. He was so proud of Helen's progress and was eager to see her continue learning, but the university seemed like too much. It was Kate's wisdom, yet again, that helped him make the right decision. She told Arthur of a recent conversation she'd had with their daughter.

"Do you know what she said to me, dear? She told me, '*The best and most beautiful things in the world cannot be seen or even touched - they must be felt with the heart.*'"

Arthur smiled. His daughter was growing up so fast.

"She also told me that our wonderful Anne Sullivan agreed to accompany her to university. She said that *walking with a friend in the dark is better than walking alone in the light.* She is ready to take on new challenges, to take a small step into the dark unknown," Kate recounted.

"I don't know, love. The university is far away, the students there might be cruel. Our daughter is so sweet and tender, I do not want her to be ridiculed and scorned." He had to be honest.

"That is understandable, of course. We love our daughter, and I felt the same way. Do you know what changed my mind?"

"What was that?" he asked.

"It was the last thing that Helen told me in our conversation. She delivered it with absolute conviction. She said, '*Life is either a daring adventure or nothing.*'"

HELEN KELLER WENT ON to become the first deaf-blind person to earn a Bachelor of Arts degree. Her life became an inspiration to the entire world and she went on to write many books and articles that reached scores of readers. She sought to make the world a better place and campaigned for women's right to vote, labor rights, and antimilitarism.

She shared many important lessons and taught, "*Alone we can do so little; together we can do so much.*"

"*Keep your face to the sunshine and you cannot see the shadows.*"

"*Optimism is the faith that leads to achievement. Nothing can be done without hope and confidence.*"

"*Although the world is full of suffering, it is also full of the overcoming of it.*"

"*What we have once enjoyed we can never lose. All that we love deeply becomes a part of us.*"

Thankfulness filled Helen's heart when she learned how to communicate. Instead of **lamenting** her difficult condition, she focused on gratitude and brought love and light to the whole world. Being thankful helped Helen rise up from the darkness. It can help us as all as well.

21. UNITY of Vasco

State of being joined together, in agreement; oneness, harmony.

"Ó mar salgado, quanto do teu sal São lágrimas de Portugal!... Valeu a pena? Tudo vale a pena. Se a alma não é pequena." (Oh salted sea, how much of your waters are tears from Portugal? ...Is it worth it? Everything is worth it if the soul is not weak.) – Fernando Pessoa

Cape of Good Hope, Africa, 1498

"**S**ecure the rigging! Batten down the hatches!" Sailors scurried across the rocking deck, trying to secure the hatch-tarpaulins before the storm tore them apart. Violent waves broke against the **starboard** side of the ship, pressing into it with such force it threated to tip the entire craft over entirely.

"Ensign Fernando, get out of that crow's nest. Are you mad, boy?" Vasco da Gama's voice could barely be heard between the lightning's thunderous claps. White-hot electricity, brighter and hotter than the surface of the sun, cracked through the sky all around the struggling vessels.

"I can see them, sir, it's one of the carracks, it's sinking, sir!" Fernando had to cup his hands around his mouth to be heard.

Cabo das Tormentas, the Cape of Storms, they were passing through the most perilous stretch of sea in their voyage. For over a year they had been forging an oceanic route from their homeland of Portugal to the rich markets of India.

Da Gama's **Lusiads** were the first Europeans to treat with the sultan in Mozambique, the first to visit the port of Mombasa and Somalia. They were the first to discover a sea route to Calicut, India without having to traverse the pirate-infested Mediterranean.

They had come so far, done so much, survived such impossible odds. Now, before his eyes, he might lose his entire fleet. None at the capital would even hear the tales they had to tell. He and his crew would be just another set of names among the thousands of Portuguese sailors and ships lost to the vast blue **abyss**.

Wives would mourn the loss of husbands, children would cry at the news, parents would never see their sons again in this life. You may love the sea, but the sea does not love you. It is beautiful, alluring, filled with promise of fortune, but it can be lethal, relentless, and infinite.

Da Gama, held onto the hull for all that he was worth. He grimaced, a carrack, that meant it had to be the São Rafael, commanded by his brother Paulo da Gama. Of their humble four-ship fleet, they had already lost one of the caravels to the ocean's unyielding grasp. Darkness prevented them from recovering more than just a few of the sailors and those few were half-drowned by the time they reached them.

"BRING THE SHIP AROUND, we are going back to the São Rafael," he called to his first mate. Rain had drenched everything, his water-logged cloak felt heavy on his shoulders.

"Aye, Captain, but in this darkness and this turbulent sea I am afraid we risk too much if we bring her about." His first mate, the second in command, was now by his side. The officer felt compelled to confirm the order. It would be a perilous maneuver.

"*I am not afraid of the darkness. Real death is preferable to a life without living.* We have already lost the crew of one of our ships this murderous night; we will not lose another. Bring her about, the São Gabriel will hold." Vasco patted his first mate on the shoulder, and then gently shoved him toward the steering wheel. "Now go, bring me right alongside her."

Vasco balanced his way toward the lifeboat and shouted orders as sailors buzzed by, the ship a hornet's nest of activity.

"Fernando, grab two men and meet me at the lifeboat. We are going to rescue our sailors, even if it means ferrying them back one by one."

"Aye, aye, sir, right away, sir!" Fernando jumped down with **alacrity** as he moved out.

The São Rafael's silhouette flashed into view in vivid snapshots, the lightning capturing moments like a strobe. It was no longer just listing along the side of its port beam; it was beginning to roll and would soon be completely capsized.

Da Gama squinted through the jet-black view before him, waiting for the next strike of lightning. There it was, the high rounded stern and large aftcastle of his brother's craft. He thought he saw a figure directing men overboard as they were forced to abandoned ship.

"Paulo," Vasco knew it was his brother. He'd recognize him anywhere, but especially in a situation like this. He knew his brother would be doing his duty as ship's captain. He would ensure all of his men made it to the water. He would be the last. If necessary, he would go down with his ship. Paulo was an excellent sailor and a proud man.

Sailing had been an integral part of their lives ever since they were small children. Their father had taken them to the port near their home in windswept Évora. He was a harsh man, Estêvão da Gama, but the boys never doubted their father's love.

"OUT THERE, MY SONS, out there is the future of Portugal." Their father pointed west, into the shining seas that extended out to the edges of the Earth. Estêvão drew a scroll from within his tunic and unrolled it, revealing a map.

The boys, fascinated, looked at the shapes and designs before them. "You see this, here? This is the whole of Europe. You see its shape, how the land forms together. Look at our country. It is at the very edge of the continent, facing west, facing the sea."

He then drew his finger down. "There, to the south, that is Africa. It is where the Moors came from."

Paulo had looked up at their father and asked, "Papa, those are the people who invaded our kingdom, right?" Vasco chimed in, "Are not they the ones that you have been fighting all these years?"

"Indeed, my sons, you speak true. I am a sworn knight to King João II. I have fought at his side in the *Reconquista*, the reconquest of our country. We fight to reclaim our land from an invading army that has pillaged our fields, suppressed our religion, and stricken our people."

Their father tapped the hilt of his sword; its scabbard slung about his hip. "This weapon serves a high purpose, my *filhos*. Yes, its purpose is to preserve the lives of your mother and sisters, to protect our land, but it does more." He looked out to the sea again.

"This sword's purpose is to unify our people as one. To create a future where instead of javelins and bows our children will hold compass and quill. Instead of war and conflict Portugal can be united in research and exploration. Our purpose is to usher in a new age, an age of discovery."

Both of the boys joined their father in looking out to the sea. "Your future is there, *filhos*. Learn, grow, train. If you are prepared; you will not fear. You must take it."

In a whisper, Vasco asked, "Take what, Papa?"

Estêvão looked down at his two young sons, so filled with wonder and potential.

"Your destiny," came the somber reply.

THE SÃO RAFAEL WAS completely keeled over. The once-powerful mast of its mainsail lie broken, floating amongst scattered debris. In the chaos of the shipwreck, a fallen torch had ignited the ship's stores of powder and wine, now flames leapt among the wreckage. Muffled screams for aid were still coming from the dark, and the storm was not yet through with them.

"Captain, we must return to the ship. The lifeboat is full. We have made more trips than anyone thought we could, we tempt fate too much, sir." Fernando was cradling one of the survivors.

"There are more out there; we cannot leave them." Vasco's mind was racing.

"If we don't turn back now, all of these men will be lost." Fernando gestured to those with them in the lifeboat. Many of the huddled sailors were already bruised, weak, covered in rashes, with bleeding gums from scurvy. The shipwreck was just another misery added to their plight.

Vasco looked from the wreckage of his brother's ship to the São Gabriel. Then he looked back at Fernando.

"You are right, Ensign. Return to our ship. Have the first mate prepare the hold for our wounded brothers. This night is far from over." Vasco da Gama stood and removed his cloak and boots.

"Captain, what about you? What are you doing, sir?" The alarm very real in Fernando's voice.

"I am not going back just yet. My brother is out there and I will not leave him. We are joined, he and I. This is not the night the sea claims him." He stood on the edge of the boat, preparing to dive.

Vasco looked back one last time, "Fernando, when I find my brother we will return to the São Gabriel. I know our sailors are worn and exhausted. Remind them that even the weak become strong when they are united." He leaped gracefully into the broiling sea, swimming hard in the direction of his brother.

DESPITE STORMY SEAS and the loss of two ships, Vasco's fleet eventually emerged from the Cape of Storms. Paulo survived the shipwreck. Barely clinging to life, tormented by the loss of so many of his sailors, Paulo still rejoiced at the sight of his brother swimming to him. Somehow, he knew his brother would not leave him, he knew it without doubt.

Vasco never did abandon his brother. Even when, a few weeks later, illness claimed Paulo's life –as it did so many of the **Lusiads**—he refused to leave his side.

The fleet returned to Portugal, greeted as heroes by an inspired people. The King himself welcomed their return; parades filled the streets with jubilation. The great optimism instilled by Vasco da Gama's successful creation of a sea route to the Indies prompted the king to rename the Cape of Storms to the Cape of Good Hope.

Vasco did not witness the warm reception; he enjoyed no wine or celebration. He remained on the remote islands of the Azores where he buried his brother at the monastery of São Francisco. Standing beside that old chapel, next to Paulo's resting place, he looked out to sea. He remembered that day with their father in Évora, so long ago.

He bowed his head. "We did it, brother. As one, we did it, we seized our destiny. Now, rest well, give father my regards."

THE GREAT SEA EXPEDITION of Vasco da Gama was by far the longest journey in the open sea and out of sight of land ever made. They traveled tens of thousands of miles to reach India, longer than a voyage around the whole of the Earth by way of the equator.

Vasco da Gama became the most famous Portuguese explorer from the Age of Discovery. He was instrumental in the creation of the Portuguese Empire, the largest and longest-lived empire in world history. For six hundred years the empire united Europe, Africa, America, and Asia.

Os Lusíadas, Portugal's national epic poem unified the entire nation just as Virgil's *Aeneid* unified Ancient Rome and Homer's *Iliad* and *Odyssey* united the ancient Greeks. *Os Lusíadas* depicted Portugal's defining moment when all of her best qualities were laid bare. It was the story of Vasco da Gama and his brave fleet.

Unity enabled Vasco's crew to endure the challenges of the sea. Unity gave Portugal the will to venture out into the unknown, and unity helped an empire scattered the world over, become one.

22. VALOR of Shughart and Gordon

Boldness or determination in facing great danger; heroic courage.

"The only thing necessary for the triumph of evil is for good men to do nothing." — Edmund Burke

Mogadishu, Somalia 1993

"Super Six Four has been hit. Super Six Four is going down. I repeat, Super Six Four is going down" the radio clicked off. The men in the cargo compartment of the MH-60 Blackhawk looked at each other gravely. Everything had just gone from bad, to worse.

"This day just keeps getting more and more interesting." Sergeant First Class Randy Shugart was crouched at the cargo door, his M14 scout rifle strapped to him. The city was sprawled out below; its earth and mud ramshackle homes stacked on top of each other. Brown, tan, and gray colors dominated the view.

"Interesting, huh? Well, that is one way to put it." Master Sergeant Gary Gordon was by his side, communicating through his headset. He was Sniper Team Leader on this joint-force assault mission.

Operation Gothic Serpent, that was what headquarters decided to name it. Gordon wondered if field grade officers had to go to school just to learn naming conventions. Overlord, Market Garden, Rolling Thunder, Urgent Fury, it seemed like they had a tendency toward the dramatic.

He and his Sniper Team were the finest fighting men America had to offer; they represented the **acme** of military skill. They were among the 160 Delta Operators assigned to Task Force Ranger, dispatched by the U.S. President to capture Somali warlord Mohamed Farrah Aidid. Somalia was engaged in brutal civil war, warlords were ravaging the land and stealing the humanitarian aid that the United Nations was attempting to offer starving civilians.

"What would you call it, Gordy?" Shugart had drawn his M14 up to his shoulder and was scanning his sector for combatants.

The only trouble was, in this fight, it was almost impossible to distinguish between armed combatants and innocent civilian personnel. After a successful capture of one of Aidid's top lieutenants, one of the Black Hawks providing overwatch—Super Six One—had taken a rocket-propelled-grenade (RPG) right into its tail rotor.

The entire mission exploded into turmoil right along with the MH-60 helicopter's tail rotor.

QUICK REACTION FORCES, moving in a ground assault convoy, were instantly ordered to the crash site. Mogadishu's debris-laden, crisscross maze of streets made for slow going in the convoy. Not only that, but it seemed like the entire city was awake and flowing through the streets. Warlords had prepared for this day and their militias were out seeking to kill Americans.

Militiamen, armed with AK-47 machine guns and RPGs, were ambushing the convoy on every turn. Far from a professional fighting force, they fired their weapons from buildings and street corners while wearing the sandals and casual attire of the rest of the population.

Shughart was engaging those holding weapons, those running toward the rising black smoke of the newest crash site. There were many within a few hundred meters of the burning helicopter, running toward the location, many more behind them. He was a deadly accurate sniper.

One shot, one kill. But even if he was perfectly accurate with every shot, he knew he didn't have enough bullets for them all.

"I'd call this situation exactly what we have been trained for." Gordon put his hand on his sniper's shoulder. "Doesn't this sound exactly like the type of dynamic scenario where there's need of some adaptable, intelligent, tenacious, steely-eyed soldiers? Old Uncle Sam has put top dollar into making us D-boys. I'd say it's time for the surgical application of our variety of unique special operations skills."

A SUDDEN LUCKY BURST of AK-47 rifle fire plinked against the hull of the Blackhawk.

"You saying what I think you're saying, Gordy?" Shughart looked up from his scope. "You know Brad and I are in. Let's get down there and help those boys out."

Gordon smiled, "Roger that, making the call."

"Serpent-Six, this is Overwatch Alpha, request immediate insertion to crash site two. Multiple bogies identified vicinity crash site. Time is of the essence. Request immediate insertion of Overwatch, three personnel, over." Shughart heard Gordon's voice come across the command net.

"Negative, Overwatch. Negative on insertion, too many hostiles in the area, insertion untenable at this time, over," came command's reply.

Gordon tried again, "Serpent-Six, Overwatch is tracking all. That is exactly why we request insertion, over."

There was a pause on the other end of the radio. The silence had to mean the Special Operations Commander, General Garrison, was personally considering the request. He knew most of his resources were headed toward the first crash site and it would take hours to assemble an adequate force to get to Super Six Four.

The second downed aircrew wouldn't have hours. Based on the satellite imagery streaming to his command tent, the crew would be lucky to have minutes before militia men killed them and started mutilating their bodies.

Still, the general knew that inserting three soldiers, even if they were the absolute finest killing machines ever produced by a modern military, would not be enough. It wasn't just hundreds of combatants they would immediately face, but the whole doggone city. It would be a suicide mission, that much he knew.

General Garrison also knew that those delta boys flying overhead could see the situation just as clearly as he. They were asking to go in. They knew the odds. They knew this would be a one-way trip. Still, there was a chance, however small, that they could reach the crew, get them to safety, maybe hole up in a building. It would be their own little Alamo. It was worth giving them the chance.

Gordon transmitted again on the command net, "Serpent Six, we do not have time here, sir, we need to get down there now. Overwatch requests insertion, time now, over."

The general himself came on the net, "Understood you request insertion. You understand the situation, son? We will not be able to get to you immediately. It will be a shoot-out, over."

Shughart listened to his sniper team leader's reply. His adrenaline was starting to pump, a heightened sense of awareness was kicking in. He pulled his gloves tight and started preparing to fast-rope. As he got to his feet, he remembered the stories his father told him as a boy.

"IT'S NOT THE SIZE OF the dog in the fight; it's the size of the fight in the dog." Shughart's dad used to quote Mark Twain. He grew up on his father's knee hearing stories of valor, stories where underdogs fought valiantly though they were terribly outnumbered. The Spartans at Thermopylae, the cavalry at Custer's Last Stand, his father was an Air Force veteran and inspired his son with stories of courage.

He remembered one particular night when his father sat by his bedside, the room still cluttered with G.I. Joe action figures and Legos. His father told him of ancient Greek philosophers. He quoted Heraclitus of Ephesus's philosophy on battle.

"Out of every one hundred men, ten shouldn't even be there, eighty are just targets, nine are the real fighters, and we are lucky to have them, for they make the battle. Ah, but the one, one is a warrior, and he will bring the others back."

The one.

That was what he wanted to grow up to become, a warrior. He would be the one to bring the others back, to prevail against any foe, to enter the fray when none else dared test fate.

"AFFIRMATIVE, SERPENT Six. We want in. We are the best chance they've got." Gordon was up and already grabbing the fast rope.

Another staccato blast of machine gunfire rang out from a rooftop just below. The rounds cut into the UH60 gunner's compartment, riddling the soldier manning the minigun. Blood splattered. He fell back, gasping in pain.

"Brad, get on the mini!" Gordon pointed to the gun, the title "mini" seemed so **incongruous**. There was nothing "mini" about the M134 Minigun, the 7.62×51mm NATO six-barrel rotary machine gun could sustain a rate of fire of 6,000 rounds per minute.

"Wait, no way, I'm going in with you two." Brad looked defiant. Shughart was already sliding down the rope.

"Negative, we need that mini. Give us covering fire and keep it coming." He clasped Brad around the neck. "We will not be able to do this without you."

SHUGHART WAS ON THE ground, already securing his immediate area and preparing to hustle to the crash site. The Blackhawk's rotor wash was a hurricane, filling the alley with dust and debris in every direction. He was glad he had his goggles on. Dust blinded four hostiles that were trying to shoot at him. With careful precision, he dropped all four of them, a single round to each face.

At the crash site, he and Gordy pulled the crew from the crumpled airframe, its hulk a gutted whale, drying out on a sandy beach. It didn't look good, most of them were unresponsive. The only one conscious was a pilot, Mike Durant, and he didn't look good. His femur was broken, probably his back as well. At least he could hold his MP-5 and cover the rear alley. He was still in the fight.

Two well-trained shooters, with adequate air support, could hold off an armed rabble indefinitely—if they had enough bullets. Shughart knew they didn't. He'd lost track of how long they were on the ground, how many attackers he'd killed, all he knew was that he only had five rounds left for the M14 and three magazines for his pistol.

Gordon was fighting at his back, covering his six, unleashing controlled pairs of 5.56mm at anyone bold enough to expose themselves to his deadly aim. His team leader was so cool, he announced when he was reloading in such a calm voice, Shughart had to wonder if they were in the same firefight.

Brad's minigun was working the perimeter. Thousands of tracer rounds turned the stream of bullets into a laser beam, cutting through buildings and flesh with ease.

"Damn, I'm hit." Gordon said it with such **nonchalance**, Shughart just kept fighting. While reloading, he glanced over at his team leader. What he saw made his heart drop.

Every Delta operator receives extensive medical training for combat trauma. He recognized the pulsating gush of an arterial bleed, it was a fatal wound, Gordon might not make it.

"Gordy, brother, we gotta get a tourniquet on that, Ricky-tick." Shugart was by his side, accepting the risk of lowering his weapon to help his team leader stop the bleed.

"Nope, I'm good, cover your sector." Gordon was still calm and deliberate, as though he was having a conversation in his living room. He was returning fire, even as he attempted to apply pressure to his gaping wound. "Don't you worry about me, you keep earning that paycheck over there, brother, we gotta hold this position for a few more..."

A group of Somali fighters charged forward, Gordon fired rapidly, but the last man got off an aimed burst before being cut down. In a millisecond, Gordon felt the rounds punch him in the Kevlar plate of his armor, then he felt an excruciating heat in his neck, and then he felt...nothing at all.

"Gordy! Talk to me man. Gordy!" Shughart was over his team leader, assessing the damage. He was still checking for responsiveness even though he knew it was too late. With his back temporarily turned to his sector, rounds started to skip across the sand all around him. He felt something slap into his left thigh and saw his pantleg turn red.

He was filled with an unexpected calm, Gordy's stoic demeanor suddenly embodied him. Shughart turned and dropped the four advancing armed thugs. He grabbed Gordon's rifle and limped back to Durant. He could tell the pilot was in excruciating pain, but he'd held his sector. The alley was filled with bodies.

"Gordy's gone, man. I've got to get back and hold the Northside. Take this." He handed Durant the rifle. Then, with a thumbs up, he offered a composed farewell, *"Good luck."*

THE BATTLE IN MOGADISHU was the fiercest fighting seen by the U.S. Army since the Vietnam War. Although it met its primary political-military objectives, it came at great cost. Two MH-60 Black Hawks were shot down; 18 U.S. soldiers were killed and another 82 were wounded. The enemy's militia lost around 1,000 militiamen and suffered over 3,000 wounded. Many of the warlord's men lost their lives around the Super Six Four crash site.

Valor defined the actions of Shughart and Gordon. They gave their lives to protect their comrades. They volunteered to enter the fray knowing they were outgunned, but willing to do whatever it took to save the Blackhawk crew. Durant survived the battle as a result of their bravery. Sir Walter Scott said, *"Real valor consists not in being insensible to danger; but in being prompt to confront and disarm it."*

Shughart and Gordon knew the saying, *"People sleep peaceably in their beds at night only because rough men stand ready to do violence on their behalf."* We each must reflect and discover what we are willing to fight for, what we are willing to die for. Valor will help you to do what must be done.

23. WIT of Roosevelt

Ability to use words in an amusing, intelligent way; mental sharpness.

"Don't hit a man at all if you can avoid it, but if you have to hit him, knock him out." – Teddy Roosevelt

San Juan Hill, Cuba 1898

"With all due respect, sir, we ain't moving. Our Colonel isn't back yet and his last orders were to remain put. I ain't trying to be a critic, but what you are proposing sure sounds like madness."

Colonel Theodore Roosevelt was leaning up against the hasty fighting position, trying to convince a young captain that his idea just might work. In the absence of orders, what were they supposed to do? Were they just going to let the whole mission fail?

No!

You advance. You pursue the enemy. You gain and then retain the initiative.

He removed his wire-rimmed glasses and cleaned the lenses with his handkerchief. He was used to the parched dry heat of the desert. He missed the days roaming the Badlands hunting elk with cowboys. Here in the jungle, the heat was oppressive, but the humidity was worse.

Sweat would soak through your entire uniform. If you didn't constantly wipe your brow, beads of glistening sweat would roll down and sting your eyes.

"I see your meaning, son. But listen to me. We have a window of opportunity here and it will close if we do not seize it."

"Sir, my men are already exhausted, many of them are wounded. You want us to charge up a hill, over open ground, and attack Spain's best infantry, armed with the best modern repeating rifles, enjoying the sweet comfort of a formidable system of entrenchments?" The captain was perplexed.

"That's about the short of it, yes. Captain, *you must do what you can, with what you have, where you are.*" Roosevelt removed a glove and pulled up his sleeve, exposing a jagged scar.

"How did you get that?" The **lure** sparked curiosity in the soldier.

"When I was Governor of New York City, I made it a routine to walk the beat with my police officers. Some of them are among my Rough Riders right over there." He gestured over his shoulder with his thumb.

"Well, one night, we happened upon a gang fight in an alley off of Madison Avenue. There must have been twenty of them, armed with knives and crowbars. Did the police cower or walk away? No, of course not, they got in there and they did their duty."

He raised his fist and flexed a powerful scarred forearm. "Even got this little souvenir to remember the moment."

"*In any moment of decision, the best thing you can do is the right thing. The worst thing you can do is nothing.*" Roosevelt replaced his glove and looked over at the line of soldiers.

Huddled behind makeshift cover, they looked exhausted and scared. "*Courage is not having the strength to go on; it is going on when you don't have the strength.*"

The captain persisted, "Sir, I believe you, it does make sense for us to continue the attack if the Spaniards were able to halt General Lawton's division. They were the decisive operation, after all. Still, many of the men think a charge would be suicide, that we would never be successful." He looked down.

ROOSEVELT POUNDED THE earth with enthusiasm, "Listen, Captain, *it is not the critic who counts; not the man who points out how the strong man stumbles, or where the doer of deeds could have done better.*"

With finger and thumb he lifted the captain's chin, "*The credit belongs to the man who is actually in the arena, whose face is marred by dust and sweat and blood; who strives valiantly; who errs, who comes short again and again, because there is no effort without error and shortcoming; but who does actually strive to do the deeds; who knows great enthusiasms, the great devotions; who spends himself in a worthy cause; who at the best knows in the end the triumph of high achievement, and who at the worst, if he fails, at least fails while daring greatly, so that his place shall never be with those cold and timid souls who neither know victory nor defeat.*"

"Yes, sir, but it won't be easy getting these men out from behind cover, the Spaniards are raking the ground with fire all around us." The captain was regaining confidence.

"*Nothing in the world is worth having or worth doing unless it means effort, pain, difficulty... I have never in my life envied a human being who led an easy life. I have envied a great many people who led difficult lives and led them well.*" Roosevelt was not preaching; he was just being honest.

The captain was almost convinced, "What do you mean?"

"I mean, son, that *never throughout history has a man who lived a life of ease left a name worth remembering.*"

Renewed vigor filled the soldier. "We are with you, sir; we will take that hill. I will order my men to stand ready, we await your signal."

Roosevelt stood up and clapped, "Right then, good man. We move at once." He grabbed the reigns of his trusty horse, Texas, and rose up into the saddle. He drew his sword and rode back to his line of Rough Riders.

"LET'S GO, BOYS, ENOUGH lollygagging. That hill ain't gonna go and secure itself now is it?" He arrived at his line with bluster.

His Rough Riders were a striking bunch. The 1st United States Volunteer Cavalry was unlike any other military outfit. Professional and amateur athletes, upscale gentlemen, cowboys, frontiersmen, Native Americans, hunters, miners, prospectors, former soldiers, tradesmen, and sheriffs made up the ranks.

The eclectic bunch assembled just a few months after the sinking of the U.S.S. Maine. President McKinley called for 125,000 volunteers to join the war effort and Roosevelt was among many who responded. Roosevelt was serving as Assistant Secretary of the Navy at the time, but he resigned without hesitation.

The Rough Riders were distinctive in more ways than just the occupations of her volunteers. Their very uniforms were unique. Contrasted with the drab conventional army uniforms, Roosevelt's Cavalry looked like cowboys with a slouch hat, blue flannel shirt, brown trousers, leggings, and boots, with handkerchiefs knotted loosely around their necks.

"Ready!" Roosevelt rode up and down the line, seemingly oblivious to the bullets zinging by. "Forward!" He pointed his saber in the direction of the Spanish position and rode Texas toward the sound of the guns. His men cheered as they followed him into the very mouth of danger.

Their advance was deliberate and unstoppable, men fell here and there, but the advance continued **unabated**. They were almost to the top of the hill when Roosevelt saw a few men slowing down and then cowering in a crater blasted by Spanish artillery. He rode over to them, still atop Texas.

"Everything alright lads? You haven't twisted an ankle, have you?" He reigned up next to them.

"There's too many of them, sir. It's too far for us to go. It's an impossible task, taking that hill." They were cradling their .30 caliber 1896 Carbines to their chests.

"*We cannot do great deeds unless we are willing to do the small things that make up the sum of greatness.*" He sheathed his sword and drew his pistol. "I'm not asking you to take the whole hill yourself boys, just get up there one step at a time. The regiment is going to take this hill together. Now, let's go."

Roosevelt rode foreword, firing his pistol as he went. He didn't even need to look back, he was sure his men were following him. He knew that when you believe you can you are already halfway there.

AT THE END OF THE FIERCE battle, the Rough Riders took the hill. Tragically 200 soldiers were killed and 1,000 were gravely wounded, but it was the turning point of the war.

Within weeks, the Spanish fleet fled Cuba and America was victorious.

Roosevelt was a renaissance man of masculinity. He was a cowboy, a boxer, a soldier, a statesman, a scholar, a zoologist, and above all a lifelong learner. He graduated from Harvard and walked the halls of the Nation's Capital. Though he was a sickly child that struggled with asthma, he overcame his health struggles by living a rigorous life.

He earned the titles of governor, representative, and president, but most people referred to him as "Teddy." Roosevelt despised the moniker, he far preferred to be called "The Colonel." The charge up San Juan Hill was a defining moment in his life.

Roosevelt's wit and wisdom captivated the nation. He exhorted, *"Life brings sorrows and joys alike. It is what a man does with them—not what they do to him—that is the true test of his mettle."*

"Far and away the best prize that life has to offer is the chance to work hard at work worth doing."

"There are many qualities which we need in order to gain success, but the three above all—for the lack of which no brilliancy and no genius can atone—are courage, honesty and common sense."

"When you're at the end of your rope, tie a knot and hold on."

"People don't care how much you know until they know how much you care."

"Keep your eyes on the stars, and your feet on the ground."

"If you could kick the person in the pants responsible for most of your trouble, you wouldn't sit for a month."

"Speak softly and carry a big stick; you will go far."

Wit enabled Roosevelt to craft memorable **aphorisms** that helped drive people to fulfill their potential. His breadth of life experience and keen intellect helped him make and share his pithy observations. Develop your wit like "The Colonel" who took San Juan Hill.

24. XENIAL Alexander the Great

Hospitable, especially to visiting guests or foreigners; friendly host.

"Whatever possession we gain by our sword cannot be sure or lasting, but the love gained by kindness and moderation is certain and durable."
– Alexander the Great

Kandahar, Afghanistan 328 BC

Alexander entered the conquered city in an ornate white chariot, drawn by four Arabian warhorses. Locals lined the streets and welcomed him and his Army as a spectacle, unlike anything they had ever witnessed. The streets were carpeted by millions of brilliant pink and red petals of the poppy flower.

His companion cavalry rode in behind him, led by their commander and his closest friend, Hephaestion. Their shields and armor glinted in the sun even as their capes billowed behind them. The dry fresh air refreshed them as they peered out from behind bronze helmets.

It had been almost ten years of campaigns against various armies and empires. Alexander and his Macedonian army of fewer than 50,000 men were yet undefeated and there seemed no limit to what their King could do. Hephaestion still remembered the day King Phillip II, Alexander's father, predicted his son's illustrious future.

When they were both ten years old, a Thessalian trader brought a horse to Macedon. It was a muscled Arabian stallion of the purest black. Its dark mane and jet-black coat lacked even the slightest blemish, but its temperament was violent and unpredictable. None were able to mount it, even the King's best trainers. He was about to turn the trader away when Alexander asked his father for the horse.

His father scoffed, "My son, you are too young to die under the hoofs of this wild beast."

Alexander insisted, and his father gave him a chance. The young prince noticed that the horse was startled of its own shadow. So, he faced the horse into the sun and moved slowly, willing his calm into the giant steed. With great care, he mounted the horse and rode forward, careful to keep the animal's shadow out of sight. Phillip and all those gathered could not believe their eyes.

Suddenly filled with pride for his son's courage and drive, the Macedonian King announced aloud, *"My boy, you must find a kingdom big enough for your ambitions. Macedon is too small for you."*

Alexander named the powerful warhorse Bucephalas and rode the stallion into every battle. The charger pulled his chariot even now.

Hephaestion knew, way back then, that King Phillip II was right about Alexander's potential. He had personally witnessed Alexander march to the farthest reaches of the known world and emerge victorious again and again. The great warrior led from the front, marching with his men through vast deserts so he too could experience their fatigue and know how far to push them. He accepted no luxury or treat that his men could not themselves enjoy.

In battle, none were more fierce or courageous than he. Their king was the first over the battlements in a siege, and the first to meet the enemy in a cavalry charge.

Wounded over and over again, Alexander's skin was a patchwork of scars, badges emblazoned upon his limbs, marks of his audacity and contempt for death.

"*Glory crowns the deeds of those who expose themselves to toils and dangers.*" Alexander did not just believe that—he lived it.

What impressed Hephaestion the most, though, was not Alexander's prowess on the field of battle. It was his ability to consolidate the gains his men fought for, his ability to stabilize a war-torn land and return it to prosperity.

HE REMEMBERED THE WORDS he shared at the last council of generals right before they entered the city of Alexandria in this mountainous land. The king had called the local magistrates and regents to join the meeting of his key leaders, indeed contrary to the practice of killing off the defeated empire's rulers.

"*There are no more worlds to conquer. Now that the wars are coming to an end, I wish you to prosper in peace. May all mortals from now on live like one people in concord and for mutual advancement.*" He walked over to a map stretched out inside the tent and inspected it coolly.

"*Consider the world as your country, with laws common to all and where the best will govern irrespective of tribe. I do not distinguish among men, as the narrow-minded do, both among Greeks and Barbarians. I am not interested in the descendance of the citizens or their racial origins. I classify them using one criterion:*"

Alexander turned from the map and looked at his audience intently.

"Their virtue."

He continued, *"For me, every virtuous foreigner is a Greek and every evil Greek worse than a Barbarian. If differences ever develop between you, never have recourse to arms, but solve them peacefully. If necessary, I should be your arbitrator."*

Alexander respected the traditions and mores of the people he conquered. He encouraged trade and intermingling of ideas. Some warned that his reach had extended too far, that uniting a kingdom so vast was an impossible task.

His response, *"There is nothing impossible to him who will try."*

THE PROCESSION OF SOLDIERS and cavalry was at the heart of the city and Alexander dismounted his chariot. Hephaestion and the king's guard joined him as he ascended the steps of the central palace. As they walked, he turned to his friend and asked, "What are your thoughts of this land, old friend?"

His general replied **sardonically**, "Well, it is warm and dry like Greece. Alas, I do not hear the laughter of my children nor the voice of my wife, so I find this place a foul mirror of our homeland."

Short, stocky and tough, Alexander was **unperturbed**, laughing that easy laugh which endeared him to so many. "You would do well to remember the words of my gray-bearded teacher, Aristotle. *'Happiness depends upon ourselves.'* You will make it home to your family soon enough. You are not the only one who longs for Greece."

His general nodded and Alex continued. "I find the land entrancing; I have never seen such mighty snow-capped peaks. This empire and its bounty are the fruits of our conquest. But still, my treasure lies in my friends."

Alexander put his arm around the shoulders of his most trusted general, his boyhood friend. "You know what else my old teacher taught me?"

"What might that be Alex?" Hephaestion was smiling now as well. The companionship of his comrade staving off some of the pain of homesickness.

"Aristotle asked me, *'What is a friend?'* After allowing me to think on it, he answered his own question. *'A single soul dwelling in two bodies.'* You know what, General, after all these years I think I finally understand what he meant."

"I am honored to call you friend, sire. The road you've walked has been fraught with challenge, but you emerged an even better man than when you started down this path."

His king looked honestly flattered by the comment. "Yet one more thing Aristotle taught me comes to mind. He said, *'It is not one swallow or a fine day that makes a spring, so it is not one day or a short time that makes a man blessed and happy.'* He tried to teach me that *we are what we repeatedly do. Excellence, then, is not an act, but a habit."*

They reached the tops of the steps and looked out on the sweeping vista before them. Mountains rose from the ground like giants and the bright pink sands of the Registan Desert lined the horizon.

"You and the rest of our Macedonian Army have repeatedly fought against insurmountable odds, endured harrowing trials, and remained true to your duties. I've long held that *upon the conduct of each depends the fate of all.*"

Alexander unsheathed his sword and stared at the blade, chipped and war-torn. He stared at his reflection in its mirrored surface and saw his own eyes looking back at him, one eye dark as the night and the other blue as the sky.

"The phalanx is only as strong as its weakest shield. Our formations were filled with strong wills and strong shields. Our excellence was a result of each man doing his duty, giving his all to our cause."

Hephaestion agreed, "Yes, sire, and it was your leadership that gave them purpose. At Gaugamela our army of 40,000 faced Darius's Persian masses of more than 250,000. Ten to one we faced them, and yet you led the very charge with the companion cavalry that exposed Darius's center."

"When the enemy's 15 war elephants and 40,000 Cavalry smashed against our lines, our troops held because they saw their leaders standing with them. Even when 200 **scythed** chariots threated to dismember our phalanx at the knees it was adaptable leaders who opened lanes to allow the chariots to pass through the phalanx and be cut down from behind." Hephaestion drew his sword and held it next to Alexander's.

"When our Phalanx advanced, bristling with spears, and flanked by the companion cavalry, Darius was filled with terror and fled. The Persians lost their leader and they broke. We slew them until our arms burned with fatigue. We killed 47,000 and captured another 200,000 all because their god-king broke and ran." He rotated his blade, light reflecting off its scratched surface.

"These swords are indistinguishable, both blades chipped and worn, but they have tales to tell. Whatever excellence was earned during the forging of this empire, it was earned together."

Hephaestion knew the friend beside him, the warrior, the king, the conqueror, agreed.

ALEXANDER THE GREAT and his brave Macedonian Army conquered the whole of the known earth, all before he reached the age of thirty. His lifelong friendship with Hephaestion was likened to the warrior-bond of Achilles and Patroclus in mythology. Undefeated in battle, his disparate empire stretched from Greece to northwestern India.

As savvy a statesman as he was a general, he taught, *"When we give someone our time, we actually give a portion of our life that we will never take back."*

"I am not afraid of an army of lions led by a sheep; I am afraid of an army of sheep led by a lion."

"Let us conduct ourselves so that all men wish to be our friends and all fear to be our enemies."

Alexander chose to be xenial with his people. He gave them freedom and allowed them to rule themselves as much as possible. His benevolence earned him their loyalty until the day he passed from this life. Be a friendly host.

25. YOUTHFULNESS of Mothers

Vigor, freshness, and vitality as associated with being young.

"Motherhood is crazy and chaotic. It's survival of the fittest most days. I've learned kids can either give you grey hairs or spark youthfulness inside you. It's up to you how you want to age." -Sara Allen

Fort Leavenworth, Kansas 2018

"Come play with me, Daddy." His daughter, Journey, was at his side again, begging for attention. "Please Daddy, I want you to play with me. We can play Barbies or we can jump outside. Play with me."

The blond-haired four-year-old was using every ounce of her powers of persuasion. Her shining, sky blue eyes were wide with the possibility of having her father's absolute attention. Sure, she could go and play by herself, she was known to **sequester** herself for hours with her precious dolls. But her dad was home from work, and this was her moment.

The only trouble was, her daddy was exhausted—utterly and completely. He knew he should get up from the couch, but it felt so good to just slump into the soft embrace of the cushions and let the cares and stresses of work melt slowly away.

He knew there was nothing wrong with a bit of relaxation. Since early that morning, before the sun was even up, he was out there earning a paycheck for the family, taking care of business. That was the man's job.

A man's gotta do what a man's gotta do.

Certainly, playing with Barbie's wasn't in the job description for a father. It wasn't wrong, of course, playing with his daughter. But if he was choosing between the plush comfort of a leather couch and trying to keep up with a four-year-old as her imagination ran wild, the choice was not entirely clear.

"Journey, let daddy rest. I will play with you. What do you want to do first?"

His wife—Sara—stepped away from the kitchen sink and followed their daughter, who was practically squealing with excitement. "You relax, Babe, I got this."

He watched her walk away, hand-in-hand with their daughter. A hint of shame started to build in the back of his mind. He tried to mentally stamp it out and snuggle deeper into the couch. Doggone it. He was tired; he earned the right to sit down.

Then again, Sara had been busy too. If he was being honest with himself, her day was probably more physically taxing than his own.

Sara had just finished her third session of tumbling classes and every muscle in her body must have ached from spotting back-handsprings, flips, and cartwheels. Her shoulders probably burned especially hard after hefting child after child up onto the rings.

Physically demanding work, to be sure, but he knew she loved it. She loved seeing the bright smiles of her students when they did a bridge or a handstand for the first time. Pride would beam from their chests, and they would rush to their parents to show off their new skill at the end of class.

He could tell she found great joy in coaching, that it felt like a calling to her. How she managed the energy to keep up with entire classes of children—plus her own—was beyond him.

NO DOUBT ABOUT IT, he was lucky to have her. Sara never wanted to marry a military man. She understood that military life requires frequently uprooting your family and many months—sometimes a year at a time—of separation from your spouse. She would have to put her own career goals on hold and learn how to integrate into new communities. True, it might be an adventure, but it could also be a long and lonely road.

Despite it all, Sara chose love and entered a thrilling new chapter in life. She was determined to have a positive attitude and make the most of her situation. Such perspective helped her brave the stormy experiences that soon befell her. For within the year she had been uprooted from her hometown, moved across the country to lower Alabama, and to top it all off, endured a miscarriage while her husband was away training.

She was a fighter though, and kept her chin up through the tough times. She embraced military life and motherhood, even managed to start a gymnastics business. A few years later she discovered she had some health issues that were going to make mothering and coaching a bit more difficult. Her younger years of feeling spry and energetic seemed like they were coming to an end. It all happened after the birth of their fifth child.

Their sweet baby girl was the miracle Sara had been waiting for. They already had four strapping boys, but Sara had longed for a baby girl ever since the beginning.

During her pregnancy with Journey, she felt strong, even continued doing her powerlifting routines with a pregnant belly. Many of her friends at the gym gave her accolades for staying fit when morning sickness and nausea understandably caused many women to put physical training on hold.

He kind of felt like Sara was invincible, at least a little bit. Her first pregnancy had required a cesarean operation. They always wanted a big family; both loved the idea of their children growing up to be best friends. The medical community frowned on multiple cesareans, so for her second child, she attempted a regular delivery. Well, the umbilical cord wrapped around the little guy's neck and the neonatal crew had to whisk her off for an emergency cesarean. Luckily, everything worked out.

Sara was worried that the surgeries were going to permanently limit her ability to engage in rigorous physical activity. She was a tumbler and a life without back handsprings and flips daunted her.

With her third pregnancy, though advised to the contrary, she had a successful V-back delivery of a beautiful baby boy. Then, just a few years later—while he was deployed to combat no less—she had another successful V-back and was up and back to her regular duties the very next day.

When his wife found out her fifth pregnancy was a baby girl, Sara knew it was what she had long awaited. The family would be whole and complete. After the delivery, while holding Journey in her arms, she again felt the purest love found in life.

It was the love of a mother.

NOW SHE WAS WALKING up the stairs with their daughter, about to play barbies with that same little girl. Despite the constant demands of being a mother, despite the fatigue she was constantly fighting, despite all the energy she had just put into running her tumbling business, she put down the dishes and chose to play barbies.

His hint of guilt started to turn into a pinch.

He remembered his own mother. How had she done it? She had eight children and somehow managed to keep up with all of their busy schedules. His youngest brother had Down Syndrome and with that came a whole host of medical appointments and evaluations. She never complained about that either.

Myriad examples of amazing women came to mind. Mothers that chased after children, helped provide for the family, cooked delicious meals, kept things tidy, and ran the schedules, all flashed before him. They seemed so filled with vitality and drive.

He could hear the distant giggles of Journey and Sara. They were enjoying their moment together. The four boys suddenly burst through the back door and charged up the steps toward their sister's room, a raucous pack of wildlings.

Their energy and youthfulness crept into him, bit by bit. That pinch of guilt and shame that had him reconsidering his place on the couch transformed into a desire to not miss out on this moment.

Childhood is fleeting, a golden moment of innocence that gleams brightly against the dull monotony of adulthood. He didn't want to let this time sneak past him; he knew these kids would be grown in a flash.

He got up from his seated position and started for the stairs, the sound of giggles guiding him forward. It was time to tap back into the child inside and find joy in the little things.

SARA'S EXAMPLE AS A mother was a stand-out, shining model of how to keep that inner fire of youthfulness burning. As Mae West said, *"You are never too old to become younger."*

As stalwart as Sara's example was, she was not the only one who retained her youth, countless women the world over labored in the essential work of motherhood and lovingly chased after children even as they fulfilled their assorted duties.

Franz Kafka shared that *"Youth is happy because it has the capacity to see beauty. Anyone who keeps the ability to see beauty never grows old."* Mothers have a keen ability to appreciate and nurture beauty all around them.

Many of the prominent figures in history give their mothers credit for helping them fulfill their potential. George Washington said, *"My mother was the most beautiful woman I ever saw. All I am I owe to my mother. I attribute my success in life to the moral, intellectual and physical education I received from her."*

Marcus Aurelius gave tribute to his mother when he said her example taught him, *"piety and generosity, and to abstain not only from doing wrong but even from contemplating such an act; and the simplicity too of her way of life, far removed from that of the rich."*

Abraham Lincoln stated, *"All that I am, or hope to be, I owe to my angel mother."*

Angelic mothers the world over often exhibit a youthfulness that can only be regarded as miraculous when considering how stretched thin they are. Children may be demanding, but they also bring with them an innocence and idealism from which we all can learn. Let us be filled with wonder and vitality like children. Let us be youthful as mothers.

26. ZEAL of Earhart

Great energy or enthusiasm in the pursuit of a cause or an objective.

"Never interrupt someone doing something you said couldn't be done." – Amelia Earhart

Somewhere over the Pacific Ocean, 1932

Ice was starting to form on the instrument panel's steam gauges. Tiny crystal snowflakes rimmed the edges of her attitude indicator, miniature kaleidoscopes refracting light. Fierce polar winds made the aircraft shake and rattle.

"Stay awake. Focus. You cannot let your guard down." Amelia Earhart was squinting at the instruments. Her eyes were watering due to the brutal cold and now frost was starting to form on her eyelashes and cheeks. The words of encouragement came out slurred. Deliriousness was taking its toll, undetectably chipping away at her crisp focus and well-trained touch on the controls.

"Heading of one-two-zero, wings level, airspeed 165 knots indicated," she forced herself to keep up her scan. Fatigue begged her to close her eyes, to succumb to the overwhelming urge to rest, just for a second. Including her prep for takeoff, she hadn't slept in more than 24 hours, the last 14 of which were spent in the absolute solitude of her cockpit.

She shivered beneath her leather jacket. Amelia remembered purchasing it years before. It was her first attempt to fit in among the aviators that she so admired. She had scrimped and saved to afford the leather garment—it was a symbol of her aviation ambition. Wanting it to look worn in and seasoned, she recalled sleeping with the jacket every night for weeks.

Slow, shallow breaths turned into mist before her and fogged the cockpit windscreen. She had to reach forward and clear off the moisture before it froze solid. Amelia was flying instruments, she had to trust what the gauges were telling her, but there was something reassuring about seeing the actual horizon, even if it was just an endless line splitting soft blue sky from dark blue sea.

Her fuel indication was looking odd. With a confused look, she slowly reached up and clumsily tapped on the indicator's screen. The needle jostled with each touch. She tried to run some simple math to confirm her fuel consumption numbers, but the answers were escaping her. Her energy was sapped, the very synapses of her brain unwilling to fire in sequence.

Amelia's eyelids slowly slid shut.

SUDDENLY SHE WAS WALKING along a grassy patch of ground with her sister, Grace. Amelia called her Pidge; she was her very best friend. They were children again, skipping as they approached the airfield.

"Meeley, look, look at that. Do you see it, up there in the sky? It's an aero-plane. Look at it." Amelia always loved the way Pidge said her name.

"Unbelievable, look at it up in the sky, just like a giant bird. How marvelous." Amelia was truly awed by the sight.

Their mom was trying to catch up to her exuberant daughters, "Wait for me young ladies. You promised not to run off if I brought you to the show."

Amelia looked back at her mom and then squealed with excitement, "Can you believe it, Mom, look at that plane, it just did a loop-de-loop. For real, Mom, no kidding." She extended her arms and began to run with Pidge, imitating the flight path of the aircraft flying overhead.

"It really is something amazing, isn't it? I marvel at what mankind can do when it applies itself." She took a seat in the grass and leaned back to look up at the airplanes buzzing through the clouds overhead. "Come take a seat, girls. I want to speak with you."

"Awe, okay, Mom, but we want to walk over and see the planes on the ground after. Can we, pretty please?" Amelia and Grace sat down on either side of their mother and joined her in observing the heavens.

Their mother saw a moment to teach her daughters a lesson and was not going to let it slip past her. "Do you know why I brought you here?"

"Because you wanted to show us the airplanes, of course," Pidge replied matter-of-factly.

She chuckled, "Yes, of course, that was part of it. But I also wanted to show you that there are no limits to where we can go. For centuries humans believed the Earth was flat, then sailors like Vasco da Gama, Columbus, and Amerigo Vespucci set sail into the unknown and proved it was round."

"For centuries many said that humans were not meant to fly, that such ventures were a fool's errand, that we should be content to remain on the ground." She gestured upward, "Now look at us, we not only fly, but airships carry passengers to destinations. Who knows, one day we may even reach the moon."

"The moon? Mom, now you are just being silly." Amelia rolled her eyes.

"No, I mean it. Listen to me, nothing is impossible. Do you know what our neighbors say about me? They say that I am not raising my girls right, that I'm failing to raise ladylike girls. They think I shouldn't let you run around outside, climb trees, hunt rats with a rifle, or go sledding. They even balk at the fact that I let you wear shorts and sneakers." She leaned forward and rested her arms on her knees.

"Well, do you know what I say? I say *I am not trying to raise nice little girls.*" She stood up and looked down at her two wide-eyed listeners.

"Nope, I'm not raising girls that are going to be satisfied with ruffles and bows. I'm raising girls who are going to grow up and change the world. *Women, like men, should try to do the impossible. And should they fail, their failure should be a challenge to others. Never do things others can do and will do, if there are things others cannot do or will not do.*" Their mom seemed so serious.

"Listen closely. There is nothing that you can't do. Nothing. Don't ever let anyone tell you otherwise. Never take the easy path, never be satisfied with the status quo. Find your passion and pursue it, relentlessly." She reached down and grabbed her daughters' hands. "I believe in you."

SOMEWHERE OVER THE churning sea, Amelia's Lockheed Vega 5B's engine started to rev up, it was entering into a dive and wind was whipping past the aircraft at break-neck speed. Vibrations coursed through the laminated wooden ribs of the bird's hull. Amelia's head jostled up and down, but her eyes were still glued shut, imprisoned by exhaustion's magic spell.

AMELIA WAS AT THE AIRFIELD, receiving her very own pilot's license. She was the sixteenth woman to ever earn the prestigious qualification. She took to the skies with unbridled passion; she'd found something she could dedicate herself to; she discovered what her mom told her to find. Flying was her love and her inspiration.

"*You haven't seen a tree until you've seen its shadow from the sky,*" she shared.

"*No borders, just horizons – only freedom.*"

Later, she was selected to accompany another aviator and cross the Atlantic, becoming the first woman to do so in an airplane. But she was only a passenger and when reporters asked her to comment on her achievement, she gave the candid reply, "*Stultz did all the flying—had to. I was just baggage, like a sack of potatoes.*" The reporters laughed at her humor.

"*There's more to life than being a passenger.*"

Then seriously, she said"... *maybe someday I'll try it alone.*" The reporters laughed even harder. No one took her seriously. Except for those who flew with her, that is. Other pilots who took to the skies with Amelia said, "*She was a born flier, with a delicate touch on the stick.*"

Earlier that year she announced that she was going to cross the Atlantic in her high-wing monoplane airliner built by the Lockheed Corporation. Some warned her that it would be reckless for a woman to attempt such a feat by her herself. She replied, *"Everyone has oceans to fly, if they have the heart to do it. Is it reckless? Maybe. But what do dreams know of boundaries?"*

THE STRAIN OF 450 HORSEPOWER of her Pratt & Whitney Wasp R-1340C engine finally woke her from her brief slumber. The plane was diving toward the frothing ocean below and there was not a moment to lose.

With vigor, Amelia pulled on her stick and tried to arrest the dive and level the wings. With practiced hands she methodically adjusted the aircraft's attitude, heading, power setting, airspeed, and trim. Slowly, but surely, the aircraft came out of the dive and the vibrations that were threating to pull the aircraft apart abated.

Amelia breathed a huge sigh of relief. Adrenaline pumped through her like liquid fire, instant alertness dissolved the drowsy mists that had beset her. Then, she noticed something. She wiped the windscreen with a gloved hand. Yes, there it was, it wasn't her imagination after all.

Land.

After nearly fifteen long hours of flight through winds, ice, and foul weather, Amelia successfully crossed the Atlantic Ocean. She smoothly landed her airplane in a remote pasture in Culmore, Northern Ireland. Her exchange with the local farmer made her smile. He had come to see what led to the landing of an airplane in his field—certainly a first for his family.

"Have you flown far?" He asked while eyeing the plane.

Amelia replied with a sense of accomplishment that filled her whole soul with joy, *"From America."*

AMELIA WENT ON TO BECOME a pioneer in aviation and set many records. Eager to share her love of flying with the rest of the world she became a **prolific** writer. She said, *"Flying may not be all plain sailing, but the fun of it is worth the price."*

"The most effective way to do it, is to do it."

"Adventure is worthwhile in itself."

"Courage is the price that life exacts for granting peace."

"Some of us have great runways already built for us. If you have one, take off! But if you don't have one, realize it is your responsibility to grab a shovel and build one for yourself and for those who will follow after you."

"Preparation, I have often said, is rightly two-thirds of any venture."

"The most difficult thing is the decision to act, the rest is merely tenacity. The fears are paper tigers. You can do anything you decide to do. You can act to change and control your life; and the procedure, the process is its own reward."

"A single act of kindness throws out roots in all directions, and the roots spring up and make new trees. The greatest work that kindness does to others is that it makes them kind themselves."

"I believe that a girl should not do what she thinks she should do, but should find out through experience what she wants to do."

Zeal kept Amelia Earhart focused on her goal and helped her overcome the negative influence of the naysayers. Her example of tenacity and grit continues to inspire generations. We must find our passion like Amelia and pursue it with zeal.

AFTERWORD

"Carpe diem; amor fati." ("Seize the day; love your fate.")- Latin aphorisms

Perhaps you are wondering why I selected the particular virtues that appear in this work. Of the many virtues out there, why choose integrity, frugality, grit, perseverance, and zeal? What motivated this line-up? The answer is simple.

This book is a call to action.

We live in an unprecedented time of wealth, luxury, and push-button convenience. Poverty, the world over, may soon be a thing of the past. Healthcare is reaching the furthest reaches of the globe. Wars are of limited scope and lethality. For Pete's sake, in America, obesity is vastly more problematic than starvation.

If you are cold you can turn up the thermostat. If you need to relieve yourself you can do it in the comfort of your bathroom. If you are thirsty you can drink water from a faucet in your kitchen. If you are hungry you can open the fridge and get a bite to eat. Think of that, you have a device in your home that keeps food cold and fresh for extended periods—something our ancestors would never even fathom. We get to enjoy magnificent technological advances. We pick up our phones and instantly hold more computing power in our hands than all of NASA combined back during the Apollo missions. If we are bored, we can sit on the couch, push a button, and access an infinite amount of entertainment.

Life in our day is spectacular, luxurious, and convenient. For most of us, it is rather easy—too easy.

You see, studies show that as wealth increases so do the rates of suicide. Some would call that a surprising correlation, but is it? Depression, nihilism, narcissism, and greed are all too common in wealthy societies. There is something instinctually ingrained in our tribal DNA that craves more than a life of ease. I once was told about some graffiti found on a building in Bosnia, written years after conflict ceased in the region. It declared with candor, "Things were better when they were bad."

Why were things better? Because, when we face tough times we unite and work together. We muster our courage and face the challenge head-on. Like Michael Hopf noted, "Hard times create strong men. Strong men create good times. Good times create weak men. And, weak men create hard times." We live in good times and many of us have become weak as a result. I see weakness creeping into my children's lives, I see it creeping into my own and, honestly, it frightens me. The ancient Athenian, Demosthenes, said, "Will the day come when we awake to discover that we have ceded our future liberty to current ease?" Likewise, Eisenhower rightly noted, "history does not long entrust the care of freedom to the weak or the timid." We cannot be weak.

Carpe Diem.

Seize the day. Start working to become the best version of yourself, today. We need to set audacious goals and strive valorously to achieve them. We need to make the most of the present, the here and now. My grandfather said, "Every day in reality is a little whole life and our life but a day repeated. Those who dare lose a day are dangerously prodigal, those who misspend it—desperate." The time to act is now. How interesting would *Star Wars* have been if Luke ignored Kenobi's call to walk the Jedi path? How compelling would *The Hobbit* have been if the wizard Gandalf never offered Bilbo the chance to join his adventure? Who would care about *Harry Potter* if he had set aside that letter from Hogwarts? Every hero heeds the call.

I love underdogs. You probably noticed that most of the stories herein feature an unlikely hero. Audie Murphy was initially rejected by military recruiters because of his small stature. Ben Carson grew up on food stamps. Marie Curie and Amelia Earhart had to forge their way in professions dominated by men. Leonidas and Alexander the Great fought armies many times the size of their own. Seeing a leader rise from obscurity or the grit of one who gets back up after being knocked down is inspiring. In our own way, we are all underdogs.

We all have an obstacle that we need to overcome. It could be public speaking or arithmetic. It could be taking control of our fitness or finding the courage to be more assertive at work. It could be getting your finances in order or making a plan for your future. There is certainly something out there that you are not eager to address. This book is your call to action. You are filled with endless potential. You just need to start on the path that leads to the best version of you. The path is not one of ease and complacency. No, it is rigorous. You will certainly fall along the way.

Amor Fati.

Love your fate. Love everything that happens to you along the path. Recognize that each setback is a chance to learn and grow. Roosevelt had asthma as a boy and instead of letting that hold him back, he trained every day until his lungs were strong. Washington lost battle after battle, but he never gave up on the cause and rallied his troops to ultimate victory. Vasco lost half of his fleet and his dear brother during his voyage to India, but he kept exploring. We learn more from bruises and scars than pats on the back and participation trophies. The stoic, Seneca, had it right when he said, "A gem cannot be polished without friction, nor a man perfected without trials." Face your fears, bear heavy burdens, lengthen your stride, be your best self.

Of course, never forget about moderation. The call to adventure is not a demand for immediate perfection. Take it all one step at a time. "By small and simple means are great things brought to pass." This is just your call to rise up, day by day, action by action. It is a call to stand up and begin the journey. This is the beginning of your story, now get out there and stick to **THE PATH**.

My family is eager to see you succeed. We are eager to share our experiences as we too make our way forward. We invite you to join us at **challengemyfamily.com**.

Glossary

A **bdicate** fail to fulfill or undertake (a responsibility or duty).

abscond leave hurriedly and secretly, typically to avoid detection of or arrest for an unlawful action such as theft.

abyss a deep or seemingly bottomless chasm.

acme the point at which someone or something is best, perfect, or most successful.

adieu a goodbye.

alacrity brisk and cheerful readiness.

ambush a surprise attack by people lying in wait in a concealed position.

ante a stake put up by a player in poker and similar games before receiving cards.

apartheid a policy or system of segregation or discrimination on grounds of race.

apathy lack of interest, enthusiasm, or concern.

aphorism a pithy observation that contains a general truth, such as, "if it ain't broke, don't fix it.".

appellation the action of giving a name to a person or thing.

arbitrary based on random choice or personal whim, rather than any reason or system.

ardor enthusiasm or passion.
austerity conditions characterized by severity, sternness, or asceticism.

belie fail to give a true notion or impression of (something); disguise or contradict.

berserker an ancient warrior who fought in a wild frenzy.
bolster support or strengthen; prop up.
cacophony a harsh discordant mixture of sounds.
consuming absorbing, eat, drink, or ingest.

defilade the protection of a position, vehicle, or troops against enemy observation or gunfire.

deftly in a way that is neatly skillful and quick in movement.
dexterity skill in performing tasks, especially with the hands.
dictatorship absolute authority in any sphere.

didactic in the manner of a teacher, particularly so as to treat someone in a patronizing way.

dilettante a person who cultivates an area of interest, such as the arts, without real commitment or knowledge.

ebullience the quality of being cheerful and full of energy; exuberance.

elusive difficult to find, catch, or achieve.

envoy a messenger or representative, especially one on a diplomatic mission.

eschew deliberately avoid using; abstain from.

extravagant lacking restraint in spending money or using resources.

feckless lacking initiative or strength of character; irresponsible.

fell likely to cause of capable of causing death; violently unfriendly or aggressive in disposition.

firmament the heavens or the sky, especially when regarded as a tangible thing.

forsaken abandoned or deserted.

fritter waste time, money, or energy on trifling matters.

fruition the point at which a plan or project is realized, producing fruit.

gambit a device, action, or opening remark, typically one entailing a degree of risk, that is calculated to gain an advantage.

glutton an excessively greedy eater.

Gutenberg press 15th century printing press enabled the mass production of books and the rapid dissemination of knowledge.

hodge-podge a confused mixture.
impervious unable to be affected by.
impetuous acting or done quickly and without thought or care.

incessant (of something regarded as unpleasant) continuing without pause or interruption.

incongruous not in harmony or keeping with the surroundings or other aspects of something.

indigenous originating or occurring naturally in a particular place; native.
indispensable absolutely necessary.
insipid lacking vigor or interest.
insurmountable too great to be overcome.
juggernaut a huge, powerful, and overwhelming force or institution.
laconic using only a few words to say something.
lament a passionate expression of grief or sorrow.

lure something that tempts or is used to tempt a person or animal to do something.

Lusiads meaning "Portuguese" and in turn comes from Lusitania, the ancient Roman word for Portugal.

meticulous showing great attention to detail; very careful and precise.

millennia a period of a thousand years, especially when calculated from the traditional date of the birth of Christ.

myriad a countless or extremely great number.

narcissistic having an excessive interest in oneself and one's physical appearance.

nonchalance feeling or appearing casually calm and relaxed; not displaying anxiety, interest, or enthusiasm.

oblivious not aware of or not concerned about what is happening around one.

obsequious obedient or attentive to an excessive or servile degree.

opulence great wealth or luxuriousness.

Overlord codename for the Battle of Normandy, the Allied operation that launched the successful invasion of German-occupied Western Europe during World War II.

Panzer a German armored vehicle, especially a tank used in World War II.

paramilitary of an unofficial force, organized similarly to a military force.

parole the release of a prisoner temporarily (for a special purpose) or permanently before the completion of a sentence, on the promise of good behavior.

petulance the quality of being childishly sulky or bad-tempered.

picket a soldier or party of soldiers performing a particular duty.

plague a contagious disease that spreads rapidly and kills many people.

portend be a sign or warning that (something, especially something momentous or calamitous) is likely to happen.

prolific present in large numbers or quantities; plentiful.

prototype a first, typical or preliminary model of something, especially a machine, from which other forms are developed or copied.

quagmire an awkward, complex, or hazardous situation.

raze completely destroy (a building, town, or other site).

reconciliation the restoration of friendly relations.

resplendent attractive and impressive through being richly colorful or sumptuous.

sardonic grimly mocking or cynical.

schism a split or division between strongly opposed sections or parties, caused by differences in opinion or belief.

scold remonstrate with or rebuke (someone) angrily.
scythed a tool used for cutting with a long, curved blade.

secession the action of withdrawing formally from membership of a federation or body, especially a political state.

sequester isolate or hide away.

sordid involving ignoble actions and motives; arousing moral distaste and contempt.

squalor the state of being extremely dirty and unpleasant, especially as a result of poverty or neglect.

SS "Schutzstaffel," one of the most powerful and feared organizations in all of Nazi Germany.

starboard the side of a ship or aircraft that is on the right when one is facing forward.

steele mentally prepare (oneself) to do or face something difficult.

sycophant a person who acts obsequiously toward someone important in order to gain advantage.

threshold a point of entry or beginning.

transplant move or transfer (something) to another place or situation, typically with some effort or up-heaval.

ubiquitous present, appearing, or found everywhere.

unabated without any reduction in intensity or strength.

unperturbed not perturbed or concerned.

unscrupulous having or showing no moral principles; not honest or fair.

vigilant keeping careful watch for possible danger or difficulties.

visceral relating to deep inward feelings rather than to the intellect.

vitality the state of being strong and active; energy.

voracious having a very eager approach to an activity. Devouring food.

warble sing softly and with a succession of constantly changing notes.

zenith the time at which something is most powerful or successful.

About the Author

Chaz Allen is the proud father of five marvelous children. He is also a Soldier. During two combat deployments to Afghanistan as a scout helicopter pilot, he developed a passion for writing. The letters he sent home gave him a chance to communicate with his family and share experiences. Not only that, it allowed him to make observations, offer counsel, and ponder life's lessons. He wants to see the rising generation fulfill their potential and make the world an even better place.

He is a graduate of the United States Military Academy and holds a Master's degree from the University of Utah. Ranger, Sapper, Airborne, Air Assault, SERE, and Army Aviation Training gave him an appreciation for lifelong learning. His wife, Sara Allen, remains his inspiration and closest friend.

Read more at challengemyfamily.com.